Three
Greenwich
Built Ships

Three Greenwich Built Ships

DAVID C. RAMZAN

AMBERLEY

First published 2013

Amberley Publishing
The Hill, Stroud
Gloucestershire, GL5 4EP

www.amberley-books.com

Copyright © David C. Ramzan , 2013

The right of David C. Ramzan
to be identified as the Author of this work
has been asserted in accordance with the
Copyrights, Designs and Patents Act 1988.

ISBN 978 1 4456 0096 3
E-BOOK ISBN 978-1-4456-3408-1

British Library Cataloguing in Publication Data.
A catalogue record for this book is available from
the British Library.

Typeset in 9.5pt on 12pt Celeste.
Typesetting by Amberley Publishing.
Printed and bound in the UK by CPI Colour.

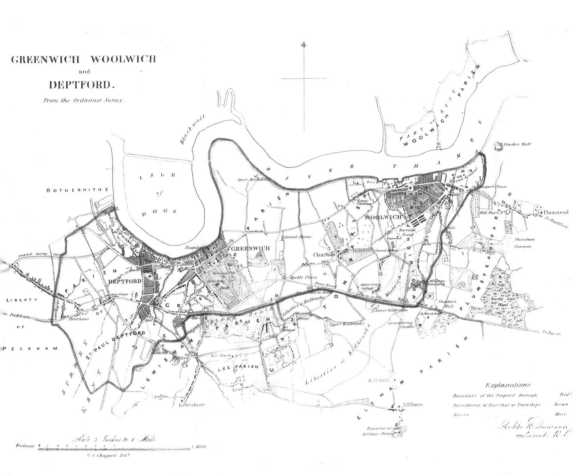

GREENWICH WOOLWICH
and
DEPTFORD.

From the Ordnance Survey.

ROTHERHITHE

ISLE of DOGS

RIVER THAMES

PART of WOOLWICH PARISH

WOOLWICH

Plumstead

GREENWICH

Charlton

DEPTFORD

LIBERTY OF PECKHAM

PECKHAM

St PAUL DEPTFORD

LEWISHAM

Lewisham

LEE PARISH

CHARLTON PARISH

ELTHAM PARISH

PLUMSTEAD PARISH

Eltham

Liberties of Kidbrooke

Shooters Hill

Explanations

Boundary of the Proposed Borough . . . . . Red
Boundaries of Parishes or Townships . . . . Brown
Rivers . . . . Blue

Robt. K. Dawson

Scale 3 Inches to 1 Mile

G. G. Chappell Delt.

5

For Alex, Toby and Elizabeth.

Without exploring the heritage and traditions of our past, we will never have the wisdom and knowledge to make a positive contribution towards our future.

DCR

Contents

River Thames, Ballast Quay
–1960s.

Longitude 0° 0' - Latitude 51° 29' and all points North, South, East and West.

Greenwich, the nautical centre of the world, is divided through the town's centre from north to south by the Meridian line, where both sides of the globe converge. I grew up in Greenwich, spending my early childhood years playing in both the east and west sides of the world in the Royal Park and along the banks of the Thames. Living in Old Woolwich Road, at one time the main thoroughfare through Greenwich, just five minutes' walk from the banks of the River Thames, I had every opportunity to see all types of ships and boats from all parts of the world, sailing back and forth along my own local stretch of river from Greenwich Reach to Blackwall Point, although by the time I was old enough to make my own way down to the river, where my friends and I regularly played, the age of sail had had literally sailed on by. Ever since I can remember, I have always had a fascination for boats, ships and the old river industries, once all part of Greenwich life. The only opportunity we had as youngsters of seeing great sailing ships on the Thames came when the annual Tall Ships Race arrived at Greenwich. Sadly, this historic international ocean-going sailing ship competition no longer makes a call at Greenwich, since the construction of the Queen Elizabeth II Bridge – a road crossing between Dartford in Kent and Thurrock in Essex – prohibits the largest of tall ships' passage along the Thames, as the their masts are too tall to pass under the concrete and iron raised section of the motorway river crossing. Much smaller sailing craft are able to navigate up river, but most are pleasure craft, or reconstructions of historical sailing ships used for film productions and maritime festivals.

Above: River Thames, Southbank, Greenwich – 2011.

Square-rigged merchantman, with course and topsails raised on fore and main masts.

With generations of family descendents born and raised in the local areas of Deptford, Greenwich and Woolwich, it is not surprising that many, along with their friends and neighbours, were involved in working within the riverside trades, maritime industries

9

From left to right:
Charles Ramzan, early 1900s.

HMS Victory *– 1920.*

PC Edward Robinson – 1878.

Yeoman of the Guard William Robinson during the late 1800s.

Left: *Charles Henry Joseph Ramzan – 1944.*

Right: *HMS* Shah, *escort aircraft carrier stationed in the Pacific towards the end of the war.*

and military establishments situated throughout the old Borough of Greenwich. My paternal grandfather joined the Royal Navy, but he was not a local boy and signed up in the navy as means of escaping the Indian uprisings of the 1920s. Leaving north-west India, now Pakistan, my grandfather sailed to Britain where he served aboard the *Victory* – then moored in Portsmouth harbour – which at the time, was used as a training ship for boy sailors. He later married into the Pearce family from Greenwich, whose decedents, the Robinsons, were a family of adventurers and pioneers. My great-great uncle, PC Edward Robinson, the Greenwich Bobby who captured the infamous Victorian murderer Charlie Peace at nearby Blackheath, would later take passage out to the West Indies and Canada looking to make his fortune after leaving the force. Two of his older brothers, William and John, both born at Woolwich Royal Dockyard, attended the Greenwich Hospital School for boy sailors, where their father was serving as a drill instructor. William fulfilled a military career, however rather than joining the navy or marines, he enlisted in the army, serving with a highland regiment posted to the Far East, where he met and later married a British colonial girl at Fort William, Calcutta. On retirement from the army, he was appointed a Yeoman of the Guard, serving as a bodyguard to Queen

Victoria. Another of the Robinson brothers, Joseph, served aboard the steam sloop HMS *Cyclops* patrolling the waters of the Atlantic. My father's brother, Charles Ramzan, followed in my grandfather's

footsteps; joining the Royal Navy, serving aboard the escort aircraft carrier HMS *Shah* in the Pacific during the Second World War. Another maternal uncle, Arthur Peachey, took to sea with the Fleet Air Arm aboard the aircraft carrier HMS *Illustrious* patrolling the Mediterranean.

*Union Wharf
Greenwich – 1960s*

When my grandfather died during the early 1940s, my grandmother, a Greenwich born girl, later remarried a local man George Austin, who I came to know as 'Pop'. Old Pop had been a lighterman on the Thames and would tell me wonderful stories about his life working on the river, when steam cargo ships, Thames sailing barges and the few surviving ocean going sailing ships, tied up alongside the wharfs and quaysides at Greenwich. Within his home he had a menagerie of exotic pets and unusual artefacts acquired from sailors of merchant ships who brought them into the Port of London, for sale or trade with the locals or in the back street markets located around the docklands. These creatures included an Asian monkey, Australian finches, a South American

Arthur Peachey, right, ashore on the Island of Malta with a crewmate from HMS Illustrious.

parrot and an Indian mynah bird, each coming with an exciting story about how they were acquired and the far off countries from where they came. Some creatures on show were stuffed, exhibited in huge glass jars, while other curios, an elephant's tooth, ivory and tortoiseshell carvings, oriental pipes and wonderfully decorated pieces of Chinese lacquerware which were tucked away in drawers and cupboards, or out on displayed on shelves and cabinets around his home.

In the waterfront public houses, where my family were regulars along with their work mates and friends, merchant seamen would be found selling and trading wares acquired in foreign ports, ready to come up with a lively tale about their adventures at sea, the mysterious places visited and wonderful sights they had seen. At the age of nineteen years old, I spent a few weeks working behind the bar of the public house the Pilot, situated amongst the industrial buildings and dockside on the east side of Greenwich Marsh, to earn some extra spending money. The Pilot was the haunt of Thames lightermen and watermen, crewmen from coastal traders, tramp steamers and cargo liners, where I watched from behind the bar, while pulling pints on a Saturday morning, as large quantities of tobacco and assorted bottles of spirits exchanged hands. The Pilot is still selling pints on the Marsh, however all the industries, the docksides and quaysides have gone, and today's customers are discouraged from carrying out any private trading activities.

Throughout the early years of my life, while living in Greenwich, I never appreciated how important or how significant shipbuilding had once been to the community and to the development of the area, from Deptford, through to Greenwich and on to Woolwich, as all of these shipbuilding yards had closed down. There were still a few boat and barge building yards working on the Southbank of the Thames, located from Greenwich Reach to the east of Greenwich Marsh, but all trace of the major shipbuilding industries had vanished.

For thousands of years, boats and river craft of all types and sizes were built along the banks of the Thames. During the sixteenth century, two Royal Dockyards were created at Deptford and Woolwich to build great warships, merchant ships and ships for exploration. In between the two shipyards a large projection of land, Greenwich Marsh, stretched out northwards, enclosed by the river on three sides. This barren area of marshland may well have been included into the county of Essex if it had not been saved by the Thames looping north as it passed Greenwich, then south again on towards Woolwich, leaving the Marsh positioned within the county of Kent. When London expanded, both areas north and south of the Thames were included within the city's boundaries, and the Marsh became part of South East London.

As the shipbuilding yards at Deptford and Woolwich grew in size, the Marsh gradually evolved into a huge industrial area producing all types of commodities required to supply shipbuilding, mercantile and building industries, and in the construction of iron-built ships.

By the time I was born, in the mid-1950s, all the shipbuilding

Launch of the Lady Derby *from Greenwich Marsh – 1865.*

industries had gone. The Royal Dockyards at Deptford closed in 1869 to become a cattle market prior to the Second World War, where bombing raids damaged or destroyed a majority of what remained of the docks and warehouses. Any damaged buildings which were still left standing, were later demolished during the area's regeneration in the 1960s and 1970s. In their place, new concrete blocks of residential properties were erected for the relocation of Deptford residents – including my maternal grandparents – so the Victorian terraced houses where they lived, to the south of the town, could be torn down to make way for another high rise housing estate. Where the Luftwaffe failed in destroying Deptford's heritage, the council town planning succeeded. The vast grey edifice of the Pepys Estate, built upon the site of the old Royal Dockyards, included a few Georgian dockyard buildings situated towards the north and west of the site, which had not been

Left: *Original steps at the Royal Dockyard Deptford – 2011.*

Right: *Woolwich Dockyard Clockhouse – 2011.*

destroyed through the bombing raids and redevelopment. These buildings were virtually left to rot and decay before renovation saved them for posterity, along with the dockyard's gated entrance and a set of riverside steps, the only surviving evidence of the town's maritime heritage. The name of the estate, its roads and the concrete prefabricated buildings have been given names associated with Deptford's seafaring past and along the riverfront a series of tourist information boards have been erected, however all trace of shipbuilding which took place at Deptford, has now gone.

The Royal Woolwich Dockyards fared no better than the yards at Deptford, which also closed down in 1869. During the late sixteenth century to the early seventeenth century, both the shipbuilding and armaments industries at Woolwich expanded at a considerable rate, due to Britain's growing commercial interests overseas and the conflicts the nation had been engaged in around the globe. The working opportunities had seen the town's population increase from 17,000 in 1821, to almost double that figure by the time of the dockyards' closure. With the closing down of the dockyards and then the adjacent Woolwich Arsenal beginning to lay off workers at the same time, the people of Woolwich fell upon hard times, where many families, dependent on the employment in the docks

and armaments works, ended up destitute. A benevolent fund was set up to assist them start a new life overseas and hundreds of former Woolwich workers and their families took up the offer to migrate to Canada. The opportunity of finding a new life, in a new land, was an attractive proposition for others who also migrated to Canada during the end of the nineteenth century. The grandson of my great-great uncle, William Robinson, bodyguard to Queen Victoria, was one of many to leave these shores searching for a new life overseas, where he did very well for himself, becoming an advisor to Sir Charles William Lindsay, a successful Canadian retail businessman and philanthropist.

Left: *Deptford Creek – 1800s.*

Right: *Woolwich Dockyard – 1800s.*

Woolwich dockyards also suffered from the bombing raids of the Second World War; Woolwich Arsenal was the main target, but bombs fell across the whole of the local area. In the 1960s, the dockyard site was selected by local town planners for the development of a large housing estate, where all but the dockyard gates, an eighteenth-century clockhouse block and two shipyard basins – which have been bricked in and made into ponds where anglers can fish – are all that remain of this centre of ship building.

On Greenwich Marsh the ship and boatbuilding industries continued in operation after both the Deptford and Woolwich yards closed, however a majority of the Marsh had been taken over by commercial industries and manufacturing plants producing

The Dome, Greenwich Marsh – 2010.

Greenwich Marsh – 1970s.

chemicals, gas, cements and building aggregates. When the last shipbuilders eventually closed, a few small barge building yards remained operating up until the mid-twentieth century; however, even this last stronghold of Greenwich boat and shipbuilding disappeared into the mists of time. By the 1970s, a majority of the large industrial corporations which held commercial interests on the Marsh had moved out, leaving the area in a state of decline. The Marsh was then chosen for a site of regeneration, where modern apartment blocks, shopping centres, hotels and a school were built, alongside the development of an ecology park and a huge exhibition dome, built as the central focus point of the Millennium celebrations in the year 2000.

The whole of the Southbank, from Deptford through to Greenwich and beyond to Woolwich, has changed beyond all recognition since the days when mighty oak and iron-built ships were launched from sites along this three mile stretch of the River Thames, once the biggest and busiest shipbuilding area in the world.

A World at War and Trade on the High Seas

Naval combat between the British ship of the line Indefatigable, *the frigate* Amazon *and the Frenchman* Rights of Man – *1853. (Leopold Le Guen)*

Throughout the early part of the fifteenth century, European nations had been carrying out trade transactions with countries in the Far East by way of long journeys overland on trade routes into Persia, India and China. For centuries the Venetians had traded with the Far East through Turkey and by sea across the Mediterranean; however, after the rise of the Turkish Ottoman Empire in the mid-

Shipping in a stiff breeze sailing through an estuary between two Turkish forts during the seventheenth century. (Pieter Mulier)

fifteenth century, which increased the Muslim threat to the west, these trade routes were gradually closed off, leaving European trading nations no other option than to sail on long sea voyages down the coast of west Africa, around the Cape of Good Hope and on to Asia and China.

The domination which Venice once held over trading with the east now transferred to European nations situated on the Atlantic seaboard. Huge fleets of fighting ships and merchant ships, built by these emerging trading nations, opened up sea routes across vast expanses of uncharted waters around the world.

Fierce competition grew between these seafaring nations, where the most powerful: England, Portugal, Spain, France and Holland, fought for the supremacy over trading rights and colonisation of newly discovered countries. The result was open hostilities and a series of wars breaking out, where success was dependent on the size and supremacy of that nation's naval power.

These trade routes to the Far East and later to the Americas, were continuously fought over by dominant trading nations. Portugal was the first to open up the sea trade routes to the Far East, with Spain sailing to the west, following the route of Columbus, to colonise the new-found lands of Southern America, with both the French and English fighting between each other for the rights over North America. The Dutch; a once formidable seafaring nation, eventually failed as a global power and although the Portuguese were the first nation to begin the colonisation of Africa and later Brazil, the nation lost all credibility as a dominating force, when annexed by Phillip II of Spain after the death of the King of Portugal in 1580. This left England, France and Spain to grow in strength and divide the remainder of the known world between them, through trade, conflict and war.

First known pirate flag flown during the 1770s by Frenchman Emanuel Wynne.

These competing sovereign nations, which sailed the trade routes of the world, needed powerful fighting vessels to protect their trading interests and their colonies in distant lands which

continually came under threat from rival nations, resulting in merchant ships becoming heavily armed to defend themselves against attack from pirates, privateers and corsairs terrorising the shipping trade routes around the globe.

Englishman in action against Barbary pirates – 1680.

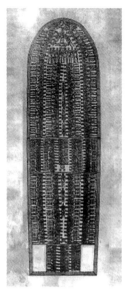

The colonisation and exploitation of new lands brought wealth and prosperity to those nations which were capable of building the biggest fleets of merchant ships and war ships to take control of the sea lanes around the world. Conquests in South America brought limitless wealth from plundered treasures of silver and gold. Luxury goods from the Far East, including fine silks and exotic spices, were bought cheaply and sold to make vast profits, ensuring that these western European nations became exceedingly rich and immensely powerful. This in turn had far reaching consequences for the native peoples of the lands colonised or conquered. The Spanish would wipe out two indigenous populations of South America, the Incas and the Aztecs, while the battles between the French and the English in pursuit for domination over North America, would eventually obliterate the Native American tribes. To the east, the English fought with the French and Dutch over trade in Asia and China, vast areas which were colonised and ruled over by these nations, with little regard for people of those lands, leading to bloodshed and death.

As the empires of the west extended out around the globe, the spread of western diseases followed; smallpox, measles, yellow fever and influenza decimated the local populations and almost wiped out whole races inhabiting isolated Pacific Islands. Throughout these times of exploration and colonisation, European superpowers would carry out one of the most despicable trades of all times, the trading of human cargo, which began in the sixteenth century and carried on into the nineteenth century, until Britain became one of the first nations to see the error of its ways and abolished the slave trade through parliamentary reforms. Along with the slave trade came western religion, where Christian missionaries set out on a quest to convert not only the slaves, but also the indigenous peoples of the lands conquered and colonised by God fearing western nations.

Sovereignty was claimed by European nations over countries which brought the richest rewards, while lands discovered further to the south and much more difficult to sail to, were used as dumping grounds for the criminal classes and a system of mercantilism was established to regulate the trade to and from these colonies, in the interests of the governing nations. Slaves taken from the continent of Africa were transported on ships in inhumane conditions to colonies in the Americas, where they were bought and put to work on the cotton, tobacco and sugar plantations by their owners. The goods produced on these plantations were then shipped back for

Plan of slave stowage aboard a regulated British Slave ship, where over 400 men, women and children were transported aboard, taken from Africa to slave colonies in America and the West Indies.

sale in Europe, making huge profits for merchants, plantation owners and ship owners, all engaged in the slave trade.

Britain was constantly in conflict with France over trade and colonial interests around the world, resulting in all out war between the two nations, which spread to the colonies in America. The British were the eventual victors in the war with France; however by the end of the war, the colonies in the Americas had become less dependent on British rule. With the French influence over America gone, there was a demand for self-government, which led to revolution and the American War of independence.

This gave rival European nations an opportunity to attempt to break British domination around the globe. The French supplied the revolutionaries with arms and supplies and then joined in with the

Previous pages: *Merchant shipping off Dover in the English Channel – 1859. (Mauritz Frederick, Hendrick De Haas)*

war in 1778; the Dutch and the Spanish – allies of France – declared war on Britain the following year. The threat of invasion severely tested British military power on land and at sea, where seaborne attacks on British held Minorca and Gibraltar escalated into a global naval war. The colonies in the Americas won their own war with Britain and became an independent nation in 1783. British conflicts at sea with France and Spain continued into the early nineteenth

Scale model of the Battle of Trafalgar. In the bottom left, the Victory *comes under attack from the French flagship* Redoubtable *with the* Temeraire *coming to the aid of Nelson's ship.*

century, culminating in Britain's historic victory over the combined naval fleets of the French and Spanish at Trafalgar on 21 October 1805, from then onwards Britain's naval forces dominated the seas and oceans around the globe for the remaining years of sail.

Although Britain had lost the Americas, the nation's trading activities throughout the world had increased after the War of Independence, where Britain had despatched Royal Naval ships on voyages of exploration and discovery into the southern oceans in the search for undiscovered continents and islands. However due to the long distances, ships needed to travel to the far south, through vast and dangerous uncharted waters; these new-found islands and continents were left neglected by the government and traders of the time. After British success at Trafalgar, trading interests now turned towards the colonies in the south, where the nation's criminals and convicts had been transported throughout the seventeenth and eighteenth centuries, as a punishment for their crimes. Through hard work and endeavour however, many of these convicts became wealthy landowner farmers and with the arrival of European migrants and settlers, a thriving colonial community developed with an economy built on the wool trade. As with most explorations to distant lands, the native population of the southern seas would also suffer from the European quest for colonial domination. The Aborigines of Australia and Maoris of New Zealand would gradually lose their sacred ancestral lands to the grazing of sheep, bred to supply the emerging and lucrative market of wool trading.

In the nineteenth century, more British colonies were seeking the rights of self-government and in 1848 Nova Scotia, which was part of British Canada, was the first to become a British Dominion, which gave the colony internal self-rule. Gradually other British colonies would follow Canada's lead in seeking and gaining self government and British influence as a colonial empire began to go into decline.

British rule and trading interests around the globe had been built upon the power and force of the nation's naval and mercantile fleets. While the ships of the Royal Navy carried out their duties of patrolling the seas and oceans of the world, British merchant ships were sailing those same seas and oceans in pursuit of trade and commerce. British sailing ships built for war, trade and exploration during the sixteenth century to the twentieth century, ensured the nation's position as a dominant seafaring world power would be unequalled. These ships not only shaped the history of Britain, they shaped the seafaring heritage of the world. The most famous of these historic vessels, *Mary Rose, Golden Hind, Mayflower, Victory, Temeraire, Endeavour, Discovery, Thermopylae* and the *Cutty Sark,* were recorded in the pages of historical literature, depicted in great classic marine paintings, built as precise scale models for

display and some, which had not survived the passage of time, were reconstructed as full size replicas. While these British-built ships became legendary, hundreds of other ships built at the yards of Deptford, Greenwich and Woolwich, during some three hundred years of British domination at sea would soon be forgotten, although many deserved the same recognition afforded to their more famous contemporaries of the time.

Saviour of the Victory, *the* Fighting Temeraire, *towed to her last berth to be broken up – 1838. (J. M. W. Turner)*

   Three of these less well known ships, one built at Deptford, another at Greenwich and the third at Woolwich, had their own remarkable individual histories, involving sea battles, voyages of discovery and record breaking sailing passages on the trade routes around the globe. Such exploits brought these ships notoriety, fortune and fame and they were written about in the popular newspaper spread-sheets and articles of the day. Initially, these three ships would have been considered no different than any of the others of the same type, built and launched into the Thames at that time, whether warship, discovery vessel or merchantman. No one could have foretold the fates or adventures that awaited these three ships after they launched into the Thames at Greenwich, sailing out across the oceans around the world during a time when Britain was a great seafaring nation and the fleets of warships and merchant ships ruled over the oceans of the world bringing the country great wealth and prosperity, which in turn also brought with it long periods of conflict and war.

Commissioned for charter by the East India Company, the armed East Indiaman *Princess Louisa*, built and launched at Deptford Dockyard in 1733, sailed the lucrative trade routes to the Far East to make the shareholders and ship's merchant owners extremely wealthy men by carrying cargoes of coffee, silks, spices and hoards of Spanish treasure.

The *Halloween*, a fully rigged iron-built clipper ship, launched from a slipway on Greenwich Marsh in 1870, sailed the China seas through some of the very worst of weather conditions, to bring home precious cargoes of tea, in sailing times rivalling those of the clipper's more famous competitors.

The Royal Naval frigate *Dolphin*, built as a ship of war and launched at Woolwich Royal Dockyards in 1751, served the nation in times of hostility and times of discovery, on the frigate's final voyage this modest little ship gave passage to one of the nation's greatest of maritime heroes.

Each of these historic sailing ships have a extraordinary story to tell of conflicts of war, engagements with pirates and privateers, of lost treasures, murder, mutiny, shipwreck and survival.

Trade winds -
The East Indiaman
Princess Louisa

East Indiaman Princess Louisa
*sailing through the Arabian Sea
– 1734.*

On the south bank of the River Thames, west of the Royal Palace at Greenwich, a small anchorage at Deptford, known locally as the Kings Repair yard, became one of the most important ship building sites in England, after Henry VIII was crowned King in 1509. The little riverside village of Deptford, once known as West Greenwich, had long associations with fishing and shipbuilding before Henry VIII decided to make the yards the site of his Royal Dockyard in 1513. His father Henry VII realised that England was in need of a fleet of armed merchant ships to protect and secure his sovereignty and to pursue English domination over Europe. Henry VII made Portsmouth, on the south coast of England, the site of the first Royal Dockyards, laying down the foundations for Britain's future Royal shipbuilding industry. When Henry VIII came to the throne, five new ships, which had been built and launched from the Portsmouth dockyard, became England's first Royal fleet. Two of these ships were large four-masted carracks, designed along the same lines as Spanish and Portuguese merchant ships, which were bigger than English-built merchant ships of the time. When equipped with deck canons and soldiers using small arms fire, these vessels became a powerful weapon for war. Henry VIII had a vision to build the biggest fleet of fighting warships that no other nation could equal, to carry forward his father's mission to make England the most powerful seafaring nation in the world.

Map of Deptford Royal Dockyards – 1623.

During Henry VII's reign, the yards at Deptford had been used mainly as an anchorage and ship repair yard and his son, young Prince Henry, would have known the yard well, born just a few of miles downriver at the Royal Palace at Greenwich where he spent a majority of his youth. The Thames, which flowed past the riverside palace, was an important water highway during Tudor times, where river craft and royal galleys travelled back and forth to the nation's centre of government, finance, commerce and trade. The Kings Repair Yards, on route between Greenwich Palace and London, made an ideal location for Henry VIII's new Royal shipbuilding yards, where the King would oversee the construction of his warships in close proximity to his favourite place of residence.

Within thirty years, the shipbuilding yards at Deptford had become one of the most important Royal Dockyards in the country. At the time of Henry VIII's death in 1547, the royal fleet consisted of forty warships all built at the Royal Dockyards during the King's reign. Henry's youngest daughter Elizabeth, also born at Greenwich Palace, continued with her father's work after crowned Queen Regnant of England and Ireland in 1558. Several of the ships that

Fifteenth-century Greenwich Palace, birthplace of Henry VIII, Elizabeth I and her sister Mary Tudor.

sailed with the English fleet in the defeat of the Spanish Armada in 1588, were built at the Deptford yards, including the *Ark Royal*, *Triumph*, *Dreadnaught* and Drake's command during this historic action, the *Revenge*.

Before Spain's attempted invasion of England, sea captains such as Francis Drake, John Hawkins and Martin Frobisher, had contributed new ideas for the design and building of faster, more manoeuvrable types of galleon for Elizabeth's fighting fleet, through knowledge and experience gained during long and dangerous sea voyages to the furthest parts of the world. Drake and Hawkins' pioneering spirit not only brought them a vast amount of sailing knowledge, their activities also brought them a great amount of wealth and prosperity. A majority of the fortune accumulated during the early days of their sailing careers came through the trading of slaves. This respected occupation brought both sea captains rich rewards, which gave them the financial stability to develop their expanding overseas trading activities.

In 1572, Matthew Baker, son of one of Henry VIII's shipwrights who had travelled far and wide, studying new shipbuilding methods in Europe, was appointed England's Master Shipwright. The experiences he acquired while travelling throughout Europe were put to good use when building a new style of galleon at Deptford dockyard. These sleek new style of fighting ships were built to formulated specifications and laid out plans, rather than by the old fashioned methods of rule of thumb. Designed with a lower superstructure, longer prows, reduced fore and aft castles and more sophisticated rigging, the new designs enabled ships to sail much closer to the wind, giving them faster and better sailing capabilities. These new innovative ship designs were a major contributing factor in the defeat of the Spanish Armada, where the English ships easily out-manoeuvred the larger, more cumbersome Spanish and Portuguese ocean going sailing vessels.

After the defeat of the Spanish Amada, England's position as a great and powerful seafaring nation was assured, with the victorious Queen Elizabeth looking upon trade and commerce overseas, along with the pillage and plunder carried out by her privateers Drake and Frobisher, as a way to increase the wealth of her nation. In 1600, Elizabeth granted a royal charter to the 'Governor and Company of Merchants of London Trading into the East Indies' – referred to as the 'Company' – granting them rights to trade in the East Indies' spice trade. The Dutch and Portuguese had once monopolised the trade to the East Indies, but now with England's emergence as a leading world power, their hold was weakened over this lucrative market.

East India House off Leadenhall Street early 1700s.

Although it had been proved that English ships and their crews were a superior fighting force, Spanish, Portuguese and Dutch ocean going fleets of merchantmen, were far better equipped when it came to sailing long and hazardous voyages to the East and West Indies. With the emergence of new trading opportunities opened through the granting of this Royal Charter, City merchants and the Company stockholders were in need of a fleet of their own ships, to better those of their rivals in cargo carrying capacity and reliability. The Company began purchasing and leasing the best merchant ships available at the time, in pursuit of the riches the spice trade would bring. These long voyages often took two years or more to complete, with the ships returning in extremely poor condition, if they ever returned at all. The severe weather and sailing conditions wrecked many merchant vessels on passage to or from the Far East, while others were attacked by pirates and privateers intent on stealing the merchant ships' precious cargo. These merchant vessels made no more than three or four voyages during the ship's working lifetime, eventually succumbing to the rigorous sailing conditions and dangers faced while sailing unknown and hostile waters.

The replacement of ships proved exceedingly costly and in 1607, the Company made the decision to lease yards at Stone Wharf in Deptford Strand, adjacent to the Deptford Royal Dockyards, to build Company ships, known as East Indiamen, rather than continue to buy or lease them. A ship of 300 tons purchase privately by the Company cost around £13,500, whereas the outlay to build a ship in its own yards cost a mere £4,000, reducing the Company's initial outlay by two-thirds. The money from the savings made were invested in the purchase of further luxury goods from the East Indies to make the Company even more profit for its stockholders, which resulted in the need to build even more East Indiamen to ship back even more goods.

With the Company becoming exceedingly rich through its trading and commercial activities, no expense was spared on

East Indiaman under construction in Barnard's Yards Deptford – 1824.

the construction of its fleet of East Indiamen, with each ship extravagantly decorated from stem to stern, setting them apart from any other trading ship of the time. Over forty East Indiamen were built during the time the Company leased the yards at Deptford and were considered to be the finest merchantmen to have ever graced the oceans and seas around the world.

The Company yard employed hundreds of workers, shipwrights, carpenters, blacksmiths, sailmakers, warehouse men, clerks, sea captains and sailors, with many living in the town of Deptford. Rows of small wooden terraced cottages, erected to accommodate the shipwrights, carpenters, merchant sailors and a majority of the less skilled workers at both the Royal Dockyards and Company shipbuilding yard, were located throughout the backstreets of the poorest part of the town.

Master Shipwrights, Dockyard Foreman and Royal Navy ships' captains and masters of Company ships, were able to afford to buy or rent the much more elegantly brick-built properties in the town's main high street, or houses erected adjacent to the Deptford dockyards. Deptford had grown into a huge shipbuilding community through the working opportunities the dockyards had brought to this once small riverside fishing village.

As the Company's commercial interests grew through its increasingly successful trading ventures to the East Indies and China, the Company began to have a significant influence over the development of the port of London, the surrounding docklands, and the capital's financial and commercial centre. The government became increasingly wary of how powerful the Company was becoming, nevertheless there was a reluctance to restrain the Company's activities due to the vast amount of revenue the government made from the customs duties levied on the imported goods.

The Company stockholders, always ready to find new ways to increase the Company's profitability, made the decision to have ships built by private owners, then enter into leasing contracts, benefiting the owners, builders and the Company. After almost thirty years of building ships at Deptford, the Company withdrew its leases in 1643 and a succession of shipwrights leased the yards to continue building East Indiamen, now financed by the vessels' managing owners.

The managing owners, the majority of whom were Company shareholders, were given the title of Ship's Husbands and they not only provided the finances to build the ships, but they also employed the captain, the officers and crew to sail them. Each ship built was required to conform to strict Company specifications on the understanding that the Company, for an agreed number of voyages, would profitably employ these vessels and set a specified fixed price for each cargo, which benefited the ship's Husband, and the Company.

When a rival company of merchants challenged the 'Governor and Company of Merchants of London' over the sole trading rights in Asia and China, the two companies agreed terms to merge to become one powerful trading organisation. In 1709, the formidable 'East India Company' was created.

The stockholders and ship owners of the newly formed East India Company set out on an unrivalled programme of shipbuilding to serve the Company's trading interests throughout Asia and the Far East. A wealthy London merchant and shipping agent, Thomas Hall, Squire of Benego, managed several East Indiamen chartered to the Company, which had sailed on many profitable voyages to the East Indies. The Squire held ancestral lands in Hertfordshire and property in London and made his fortune as a young man through his trading activities in activities in Europe, Asia and South America. Thomas Hall first went to sea as a ship's purser on the East India Company ship the *Essex*, then later as captain of his own vessel, sailing the tea-trade routes to China, making a large personal fortune in the process. By his fortieth year, Thomas Hall had become an extremely successful City merchant and ship contractor, a well-respected member of London society and an important influential member of the East India Company. In 1730, Thomas Hall commissioned a new East Indiaman to be built by shipbuilders Bronsden and Wells in the yards at Deptford, one of the busiest and most prosperous shipbuilders on the Thames.

Peter Bronsden had already become a

wealthy Master Shipwright before entering into partnership with Abraham Wells of Rotherhithe. From the money made through his thriving shipbuilding business, Bronsden had a large and impressive family house, built away from the squalor of the grim dockyards, on Blackheath, an area of open green land south of Greenwich where many of London's wealthiest and most influential members of society resided. Bronsden's business partner Abraham Wells, had also become an extremely wealthy shipbuilder through his family shipbuilding business located at Rotherhithe, west of Deptford. This well-established family-firm had been building and launching ships since the sixteenth century, receiving mention in the diaries of Samuel Pepys, who at the time was the Chief Secretary to the Admiralty.

East India Company flag flown aft on an East Indiamen during the mid-1700s. It is believed that the East India Company flag was adopted by the American revolutionaries, which later became the national flag after the War of Independence, with the Union Flag in the top corner replaced by stars on a blue background.

Once the contracts had been agreed between Thomas Hall, on behalf of the ship's consortium of owners and the East India Company and Bronsden and Wells, work began on the building of the East Indiaman under the Company's Articles of Agreement. These Company Articles were drawn up to ensure the builders conformed to the specifications and clauses laid down, relating to the ship's size, tonnage, materials used and costs to build, which came to just under £4,000. As with most East Indiamen of the period, the ship would be given the name of a respected member of the Royal Family and the latest addition to the long line of East Indiamen built at the Deptford yards was named in honour of King George II's youngest daughter, *Princess Louisa.*

The design of the East Indiaman conformed to Company specifications and would be built as a three-masted, two-decker, carrying thirty guns, measuring 120 feet in overall length, 33 feet in breadth, with a hold measuring just over 14 feet deep. Although not one of the largest East Indiamen to be built, registered at just 498 tons, the *Princess Louisa* would be one of the most beautiful ships launched from the yards at Deptford. During the seventeenth century, East Indiaman had been registered at over 1,000 tons; built to carry heavy loads, the ship weight when loaded made them slow and cumbersome to handle. In an ever-increasing quest for speed, the Company began to commission ships with half this registered tonnage. These smaller vessels were not dissimilar in design and layout to the 1,000 ton East Indiaman, however the changes made to the form of the hull, the shape and plan of the sails and the way the ship was rigged, gave these more compact East Indiamen much better sailing qualities. These smaller ships were also much more economical to build, although no expense was spared on the ships' decorations – the *Princess Louisa* would retain the magnificent intricately carved roundhouse and great cabin at the stern – which set the East Indiamen apart from other merchant vessels of the time.

Master Shipwright Peter Bronsden was responsible for the overall running of the yard and in securing the services of the best shipwrights, craftsmen and carpenters to work on the East Indiaman. The Deptford dockyard certainly offered plenty of opportunities of work, especially when a new ship was on the stocks. There were many young men from the town applying to become apprentice shipwrights at the yard, where an apprenticeship would take up to seven years to complete before the trainee was be issued with a shipwright certificate. One Deptford boy, William Penny, attempted to apply for an apprenticeship claiming he was fifteen years old, however his application was refused when it was discovered that he was only eleven. The enterprising youngster reapplied the following year, when he had grown a couple of inches in height and was accepted. Master Carpenter, John Cleverley, acquired the skills of his trade working at the dockyards of Deptford at the time *Princess Louisa* was built. John Cleverley not only became a master carpenter, but he also became an accomplished and respected marine artist, producing many splendid paintings depicting a variety of ships launched at the Deptford yards. The carpenter and artist continued working and living in the local area for the remainder of his life. On finishing an apprenticeship, there was plenty of work to be found for good shipwrights in the yards where around 150 men would be employed in the building of a ship the size of the *Princess Louisa*. Along with their regular wages, shipwrights received extra rewards by way of 'perks', where they were allowed

to sell off-cuts and chippings of wood to earn themselves extra income.

As well being in charge of recruiting the yard workers, Peter Bronsden was also responsible for ordering the supplies and materials required in the building of the ships, which included English oak, the timber used for a majority of ship construction, cut and transported from the nearby forests of Kent. Below the waterline, a ship's hull was sheathed in deal, which provided a replaceable non-structural skin to form a barrier against dreaded sea worm attack. When the Royal Navy were not engaged in conflicts of war at sea, ships under construction would be left for long periods of time on the slips or stocks, to allow the timbers to shrink and settle before the hull was finished off prior to the launch. However, private contractors building ships for charter by the East India Company were not afforded this luxury, as the owners of East Indiamen required a quick return on the investments made in the building of these ships. This resulted in the yard's workforce being driven extremely hard to ensure the ships were completed without delay, where on average an East Indiaman would take around eighteen months to build and completely fit out.

The construction of the ship began on the dockyard slip, made ready by first laying down blocks to support the hull while long vertical poles were erected each side in readiness to hoist up the heavy ship's timbers. While the work proceeded on the slip, full-size templates were made up in the mould loft, a long wide space above the yard's workshop, which were used as guides for cutting and shaping the timbers to fit. A false keel was then laid down to support and protect the actual ship's keel, which was then laid on top. Although oak would be used for a majority of the ship's framework, the keel was usually made of sections of elm, which grew much straighter than oak and were fixed together by scarph joints, driven through with wooden plugs to hold them in place. When the keel was laid on the slip, a coin would be placed under the keel block as a symbol of good fortune and safe travelling. When the keel was in position the ship's sternpost would then be bolted onto an inner sternpost that was then raised up and fixed into place.

The curved stempost, made out of several sections of timber scaphed together, would be raised into position at the bow of the ship. The keel was crossed by sections of floor timbers that were almost

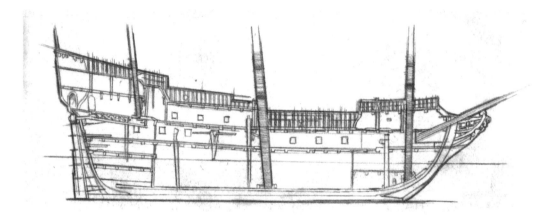

Plan of an eighteenth-century East Indiaman comparable to the design of the Princess Louisa.

flat amidships before they gradually began to curve upwards towards each end of the ship. The floor timbers were fixed into position using triangular deadwoods and the whole assembly was locked into place by laying down timber beams, called the keelson, which ran along the top of the floor timbers parallel and above the ship's keel. The frame of the ship was made up from transverse sections of timbers known as futtocks, which were bolted together to make up the complex curvature of the ship's hull. The ship's gun ports were staggered to allow every second transverse frame to continue to the upper deck with the alternate frames butting up to the lower sills. Any protruding timbers were then trimmed to shape before ribbans were fitted along the length of the hull to hold the futtocks in place.

The ship's stempost was built out to support the beakhead, a platform where the ship's crew worked the bowsprit sails and the stern would be reinforced with vertical beams attached to the timbers built up between the keel and keelson. Vertical pillars of timber were fitted internally to support the decks and with the hull completed, the galleries – accommodation for captain and officers – were then built up aft of the vessel. The decks were planked out and then reinforced for positioning of the guns and the hull was then clad inside and out with strong oak planks fitted a row at a time, starting at the keel upwards. The hull planks were laid edge to edge producing a smooth finish to the hull, a method known as carvel planking. Each plank had first been soaked before being raised into place and secured by oak nails, which were countersunk into the plank, with the head of the nail packed around with twisted oakum, tarred hemp or flax.

Although a majority of the ship was timber-built a small amount of ironware was used throughout the ship construction, nails, bolts, fixings and fastenings, all made by smithies in the yard foundry. The ship's hull was made watertight by sealing the seams between the planking and joints with oakum forced into the seams using a mallet and iron. Experienced craftsman carried out this process with great care, each taking a day to complete one hundred feet of planking. The hull was then sealed and coated in pitch to make it watertight and rigid. Finally, the bottom of the hull was painted white and the sides of the vessel were tarred. The ship's steering gear was fitted out before launch, where the long wooden rudder would be hung onto the ship's stern post using large iron rings. The rudder was operated by a large double wheel and tiller rope, new developments in ship steering in the eighteenth century, where the rope was wound around a drum fitted between the double wheel. The rope then passed down via a corner block to the tiller made up of two lengths of strong rigid oak joined as one, positioned on the ship's lower deck.

Before the ship was ready for launch, supporting cradles were built around the hull forward and aft, with groups of props fixed at the same position as the cradles. The ship was built stern towards the water, which ensured a smoother launch, as the rounder shape of the stern offered greater resistance when entering the water. The broader beam astern also helped in stabilising and settling the ship once in the water and clear of the slipway.

On the day of the East Indiaman's launch, with the tide at its highest point, the Master shipwright, Husband, consortium of owners and accompanying entourage, dressed in all their finery, took their places on a special platform built up on the vessel's bow. Everyone who worked upon the ship would attend, along with the local population of the shipbuilding town, waiting in eager anticipation for the festivities to begin. It was common for crowds of more than 20,000 to pack into the yards and along the riverfront of Deptford, attempting to try to get the best view of the launch, a spectacular and colourful occasion. In the best maritime traditions, the launch of any ship was considered the day of the ship's birth and a significant event for any member of the crew attending the festivities as they would be entrusting their lives to this new vessel; the launching ceremony bonded the crew to their new ship. Mariners had long believed that any mishap during a vessel's slide from land to water foretold disaster, however if the transition went smoothly it was cause for celebration.

At the appointed time the order would be given for the holding blocks to be released, where under the ship's own weight, the vessel gradually began to slide down the slips with the flag of the East India Company flying high over the deck. As the East Indiaman entered into the murky green waters of the River Thames, the officials aboard took a sip of wine from the ceremonial goblet passed between them all to mark this special occasion and wished good health to the ship and all those who sailed in her. The remainder of the wine was thrown down across the bow of the ship in a ceremonial blessing and naming of the ship; a tradition that dated back to ancient times when the gods were called upon to protect the ship and crew from the perils and dangers of the sea. Surrounded by riverboats packed full of people cheering and waving in joyful celebration and crowds on the shore, the *Princess Louisa* settled into the water off the dockyard slips west of Greenwich Reach, on 7 December 1732. When the celebrations were over, preparations began for the ship's fitting out, which would take several months to complete.

The masts and yards for the East Indiaman were complete and ready for fitting soon after the launch. Although half the tonnage of earlier Company ships, the *Princess Louisa* was much too big for the masts to be cut from single trees. The lower mainmast and lower foremast were built up from long lengths of pine beams, cut and dovetailed together around a single central spindle that was bolted in place and held together with iron rings and rope lashings. These iron rings, fitted while hot, shrunk as the rings cooled down, holding the lengths of timber tightly together. The ship's upper masts were cut from single trees where possible and when finished, all the masts would be rigged out before raised into position by the yard's labourers using a manually operated derrick. Before the mainmast was fitted into its central position, a silver coin would be placed under the base of the mast to bring the ship good fortune. With the masts secured in place, the yards, booms and gaffs were rigged to carry the ship's sails, which were cut and made in the dockyard

sail loft. Each sail was trimmed from lengths of cotton canvas and sewn together by skilled sailmakers using hemp yarn thread, which was tarred and then treated with beeswax. The sailmakers carried out this work by hand, producing twenty square feet of sail a day, which included cutting, sewing and hemming. Merchant ship's sails were tanned on completion, which helped prevent sails becoming covered with mildew while furled when not in use.

During the building and fitting out of the ship, a wood carver worked on the *Princess Louisa*'s figurehead and the beautiful decorative carvings which adorned the beakhead and stern gallery. The intricately carved figures and friezes were cut from joined layers of pine, then gilded and painted in fine detail before being fixed into position. East Indiamen were highly decorated to impress the officials and merchants of Asia and China, showing these magnificent vessels came from a country of wealth and power. The officers' quarters and passengers' accommodation, located in the stern galleries, were also impressively fitted out in fine dark wood panelling, expensive made-to-measure furniture and built in fitted cabinets and shelving. The gundeck was fitted out to carry the ship's main guns and to accommodate most of the ship's crew, with the boswain's room and carpenters' cabin located forward, the able and ordinary seamen amidships, and the galley, stewards' room, sickbay, surgeon's cabin, petty officers' workstation and weapons store aft. The ship's large main hold was positioned directly below the gundeck accessed by a large hatch forward of the mainmast. The ship's cable locker and sail room were positioned forward of the hold with the galley storeroom and bread room aft.

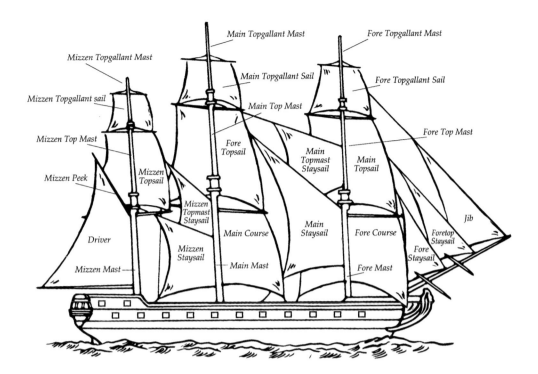

Sail plan of an
eighteenth-century
square rig ship
carrying sixteen sails.

The fitting out of the *Princess Louisa* almost doubled the initial costs Thomas Hall paid out to build the ship which took a year to complete. After the fitting out the ship was made ready for seas trials, carried out to measure the vessel's performance and seaworthiness. Once the seas trials were completed and a certificate for commissioning had been issued, Thomas Hall offered the ship to the Company Directorate for charter. A charter agreement was drawn up between the owners and the Company which was an immensely complex and detailed document covering every conceivable occurrence that may happen during the voyage, but most importantly laid down the amount of freight to be carried and prices to be paid by the Company to the owners for the returning cargo.

Sailing under the flag of the East India Company the *Princess Louisa's* commander for the maiden voyage was Captain Richard Pinnell, an experienced merchant sea captain and a good friend of Thomas Hall the ship's Husband. Captain Pinnell had first gone to sea when a young man sailing the trade routes to the East Indies and the Americas where he made his name and fortune through the trading of fine and exotic goods and through his interests in the slave trade. Between 1726 and 1738, Captain Pinnell held the position as a director of the London Assurance Company, insuring ships transporting slaves from Africa to British plantations in Virginia, Carolina and the West Indies, activities that made him an extremely successful and wealthy mercantile businessman. During the seventeenth to the eighteenth century, the slave trade was considered a most respectable and honest occupation, which made city companies and the individuals involved, millions of pounds in revenue. Many of London's well-established banking and insurance institutions were built upon the profits they made from the slave trade. The merchant traders and trading companies, which included the Honourable East India Company, were heavily involved in the trading of slaves where the directors and shareholders of the Company held interests in the trading of human cargo. Captain Pinnell would later be welcomed into the hierarchy of the Company as a director, following on from his extremely successful voyages as the master of East Indiamen.

One of the duties the commander of the *Princess Louisa* carried out would be to appoint the ship's crew, selected from a list of seasoned officers and able seamen and less experienced deck hands and cabin boys. Under the command of Captain Pinnell the complement of men for the ship's maiden voyage included the first, second, third, fourth and fifth mate, a purser, surgeon and two surgeons mates, a master gunner, first and second gunners mate, a boswain and boswains mate, five midshipmen, two carpenters, the captain's cook and crew's cook, ship's stewards, caulker and sailmaker, armourer, cooper, butcher-barber and a tailor. The remainder of the crew consisted of seventy-two able and ordinary seamen, accompanied by a platoon of forty-four Company soldiers. The ship's crew totalled around 150 men and boys. At least one third of the ship's complement was made up from well trained men who were more than capable of handling a ship the size of the East Indiaman, the remainder of the crew were untrained men, who would be used mostly during the voyage to carry out manual, heavy duty work, hauling rope and manoeuvring guns. A majority of the ordinary seamen on merchant vessels sailing to the East Indies were down-and-outs and destitute young boys, who chose a life at sea with no other prospects available ashore.

The rates of pay of East Indiaman crews varied dependant on rank from captain and officers down to ordinary seamen and boys, however all those aboard had an opportunity to increase their income through varied trading opportunities which came their way during the voyage. On the *Princess Louisa*'s maiden voyage, Captain Pinnell was paid £10 a month, with his private cook receiving £3 a month. The master mates received around £4 a month, with the ship's surgeon, master gunner and lower ranking crewmembers receiving pay equivalent to their position, the ordinary seamen and boy sailors received around £1. The crew of all British ships were required to contribute a percentage of their pay towards the Greenwich Seaman's Hospital fund, a charitable organisation that supported and cared for sick and injured seamen. The extremely hard and harsh conditions the hands faced aboard an East Indiaman resulted in many of the inexperienced ordinary seamen deciding to jump ship at the first opportunity rather than continue on a voyage for such poor rates of pay.

In an attempt to keep men aboard ship during a long sea voyage half way around the world, where the crew would be at sea for some eighteen months or more, the

Greenwich Hospital Pensioners, injured and retired mariners, during the late 1700s taking some beverage at a local Greenwich tavern.

crew's full pay would be withheld until returning to homeport with ship and cargo intact. On arrival at a port of call, the hands were issued an allowance from their pay to spend as they chose, however holding back their pay was not always enough to stop men running and replacement crew were signed on whenever and wherever needed. Replacement crew were also required to take the place of any men killed during the voyage, through falling from the yards, lost overboard or dying from contacting an incurable decease. Merchant ships sailing to East Indies often took on Lascars, Asian sailors, on arrival to make up the ship's complement for the return voyage home. During the late 1700s, communities of Lascars were beginning to settle in British ports after arriving on Company ships from the East Indies, many of these Lascars then married or cohabited with local British girls, as there were no Asian women of their own kind living in Britain at the time. Although it was not illegal in Britain to have interracial relations, mixed race marriages were looked down upon causing a lot of hostility within local communities.

Provisions served up on the lower deck of an eighteenth-century East Indiaman where able and ordinary seamen ate and slept.

The ship's mess deck, lower deck, where to crew spent any free time during the voyage. The tables could be moved and stowed away to make room for the crew's hammocks which were suspended from the beams above. The ship's guns would also be positioned each side of the lower deck, which made living conditions cramped and crowded.

Even though the rates of pay for the lower order of the crew on an East Indiaman were poor, each man aboard received a daily ration of food and an allocation of clothing during the voyage, which would be more than many were likely to have received before. A day's ration consisted of sixteen ounces of meat, beef and pork, twelve ounces of bread or biscuit, twelve ounces of meal and a quantity of fish, which was usually preserved in salt. These rations were supplemented by measures of butter, cheese, oil, vinegar, honey, raisins, sugar and dry wheat, issued at the discretion of the ship's commander. Although water was under strict ration during a voyage, the crew had a choice between a quart of beer or cider a day, or a pint of wine. Brandy was also available to all the crew, which was once again issued under instruction from the ship's commander. In addition to the stored provisions, poultry and livestock were kept aboard in pens and cages on the ship's quarterdeck.

The forty-four soldiers aboard were members of the East India Company's own private army, on transit to the East Indies to defend and enforce of the Company's trading interests overseas. These soldiers were not just aboard as passengers, they would be called upon to help defend the ship if attacked by pirates or privateers. The soldiers shared the crew's quarters on the gundeck, which were extremely cramped and overcrowded, measuring no more than five feet in height. The soldiers were issued with the same rations as the ship's crew and shared the crew's mess, where they ate at the same tables and slept in canvas hammocks slung above the ship's guns alongside the ship's regular crew. Hammocks had first been introduced on sailing ships during the late 1500s, and were considered much safer and more convenient than fixed bunks which took up too much space on both merchant ships and fighting ships. Officers, passengers and any Company officials

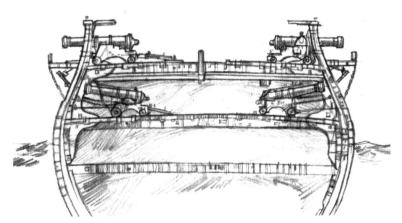

aboard were afforded the luxury of a bunk in their well-equipped private cabins aft of the ship in the stern galleries. Any passengers travelling aboard ship – mostly Company employees – were an important addition to the ship's complement, where the owners of the East Indiaman charged passage fees to transfer passengers and their goods to postings in the East Indies. The passengers aboard were issued with the same rations and provisions as the crew,

Left: *Cross section of an East Indiaman with ship's guns positioned on the weather deck and lower deck.*

Right: *Gun's iron shot, measured by poundage.*

however they would be entertained at the captain's table during the passage, which gave them some form of normality during long and hazardous voyages to and from the East Indies.

For the protection of the ship, the cargo and the ship's passengers, the *Princess Louisa* was equipped with four-pounder and nine-pounder guns, totalling thirty guns in all, with each gun allocated forty-five barrels of powder and thirty rounds of shot. Throughout the 1700s, cast-iron cannons had been used as the main armament on British merchant ships and fighting vessels, most cast at foundries in Sussex. Some ships carried brass guns, which were far superior and safer to operate than cast-iron guns, although more expensive to produce. Cast-iron guns were liable to explode on firing if loaded incorrectly sending deadly shards of metal projectiles flying through the air, whereas brass guns only split at the point of the explosion, causing less damage in the confined spaces of the gundeck for ship and crew. Even though brass guns were much safer, most ships carried the cheaper iron-built guns. A crew of six men and a boy were needed to man a nine-pounder, although it was extremely unlikely for an East Indiaman to have all guns manned at the same time. In firing the gun the barrel was first loaded with a charge of gunpowder followed by a cotton wad rammed hard down on top, after a nine-pound iron shot was rolled down the barrel, the gun was hauled forwards using ropes and pulleys towards the gun port and the gun was then ready for firing. Once loaded, a measure of gunpowder was poured into a priming pan, connected by a touchhole to the main powder charge, which was then ignited by a slow match to set off the charge sending the heavy round iron shot hurtling through the air with tremendous force. The gun's recoil would be held in check by a heavy rope wrapped around the breech, tied off at metal rings fixed each side of the gun port. The nine-pounders could also be loaded with grape shot; a canvas bag filled with two-inch round cast-iron shots and wrapped around in twine. When the grape shot was fired the bag broke open and the shot spread out causing a devastating effect when fired at close quarters against a ship intent on boarding the East Indiaman. The East Indiaman's gunners would also target the ship's yards and masts in an attempt to bring down the sails, disabling the pirate or privateer to give the East Indiaman an opportunity to make good its escape. East Indiaman gunners were mostly employed in firing signals and salutes and although they were not considered in the same class as the gunners of an English warship, they were more than capable of putting up a good fight

Ship's gun on the weatherdeck, tied off with heavy rope to counter the recoil effect when fired.

when required. A majority of East Indiamen captains would rather make a run for it than get involved in a firefight with a pirate or privateer. If the East Indiaman was outgunned and an attempt was made to board the vessel, the crew were issued small arms from the weapons store which included muskets, swords, pistols and pikestaffs. Within the Company charter agreement the crew were entitled to meet violence with violence and when carrying out their duty as expected, the crew would receive financial benefits and rewards for risking their lives defending the ship and cargo.

Blunderbuss and cutlass from the weapons store used by the East Indiaman's crew to repel pirates and privateers boarding the ship.

When the guns were in position aboard ship, four-pounders on the upperdeck and nine-pounders on the gundeck, the distributed weight above the ship's waterline would have made the ship unstable and top heavy; to counteract this, the ship was required to take on ballast before safely making sail. This would mean that merchant ships would always sail on outward-bound voyages with a hold full of cargo or ballast. On the *Princess Louisa's* maiden voyage, the holds were packed with over seventy tons of metal bars and ingots acting as the main ballast. After the heavy metal was stowed away, the remainder of cargo was loaded aboard which including bails of woollen cloth, animal hides, medicines, stationery, barrels of beer and spirits, and the most precious cargo of all, thirty large chests filled with Company treasure. These chests contained thousands of Spanish silver reales weighing around 200Ibs and with silver valued at six shillings an ounce, each chest was worth around £1,000. The silver reales were used by the Company to purchase goods or for melting down to be struck as British coins to pay the salary of the

East India Company employees and troops stationed in India.

By mid-September 1733, the *Princess Louisa* was ready to sail for Bombay. A Thames river pilot guided the East Indiaman downstream to Gravesend where the ship took on further cargo, supplies and provisions, before proceeding out into the Thames estuary, then down the English Channel to anchor at the Downs, a safe stretch of deep water off the Kent coast. Ships would sometimes need to wait at anchor at the Downs for several weeks before sailing, to make good use of the seasonal trade winds. On 4 November 1733, the *Princess Louisa* weighed anchor and made sail on its maiden voyage to the East Indies, heading south-west towards the Bay of Biscay. Once the ship was under sail, the crew were kept busy almost continuously adjusting the yards, setting, raising and lowering canvas to make the use of the best wind conditions available. The crew were often required to risk their lives when climbing the rigging to take in or let out the sails manually, a perilous activity in extreme weather conditions, where many men fell to the deck and were killed instantly. A good ship's surgeon would be experienced in treating crewman with broken bones who may have survived the fall, however in many instances, broken limbs needed to be amputated, especially after infection had set in. Any unfortunate crewman plummeting into the sea, even if uninjured from the fall, was unlikely to survive as many deckhands were unable to swim and would drown before any attempt of a rescue was made, if any attempt was made at all. It would have been extremely unlikely that the ship would be able turn around to come to the rescue of a man falling overboard before the helpless crewman was lost beneath the waves.

The voyage down the west coast of Africa to the Cape of Good Hope took around three months hard sailing, accounting for the wind conditions and unscheduled stops at ports on route to replenish stores, supplies and to participate in private trading transactions. Although contracted to sail under charter to the East India Company, the ship's officers and crew had certain trading privileges, which was the right to carry out their own private trade. Each man from captain down to cabin boy had an allocated amount of space aboard dependant on rank, for storage of privately purchased goods. During a voyage, these privileged goods were purchased when the East Indiaman made port where the ship's commander had private trading contacts. If the ship's crewmembers had the funds available, they were also able to trade on their own account, paying any extra freight charges to store goods above their allotted personal storage space. These goods were then sold on for a profit when the crew returned to homeport. A majority of able and ordinary seamen were extremely unlikely to have the funds available to take part in these lucrative private trading transactions, so they would not be averse to spending any wage allowances on small luxury items without declaring them, which could be concealed about their person and then smuggled into the country on their return – a highly illegal activity which was against Company and Customs regulations.

The *Princess Louisa* had made good progress around the Cape, entering into the Indian Ocean in February 1734. The ship was now in dangerous waters, where many East Indiamen had come to grief on the outlaying flat volcanic islands and the reefs hidden below the surface of the water, or when encountering Indian Ocean pirates, intent on attacking and making off with the Company cargo and treasure. Although ships of the Royal Navy were hunting down these pirates and raiders, merchant vessels continued to be vulnerable and open to attack. Once the *Princess Louisa* had navigated its way past the dangerous shoals and reefs, the ship made a heading of north-north-east, sailing on for the next two months towards the Arabian Sea, with lookouts constantly searching the horizon for sight of any ship flying a hostile flag.

Arriving at the Gulf of Aden, safe from pirate attack, the *Princess Louisa* proceeded steadily towards the small Port of Mocha, on the Yemen coast. A pilot guided the ship towards a safe anchorage, in readiness to unload the ship's ballast and outbound cargo before taking on provisions, supplies and a cargo of coffee. The Port of Mocha had become an important coastal market town during the fifteenth century through its coffee trading activities where regional governors controlled all the port's trading interests and the revenue made was invested back into the central region of Yemen. Local Jain, Hindu and Baniyan commercial brokers, acted as translators for trading negotiations carried out between the port's merchants, Company agents and ships' captains. The bustling, lively port, full of merchants from England, Portugal, North Africa, Arabia and India, offered a variety of goods for sale, which included spices, medicines, textiles, dyes and Mocha coffee beans, cultivated and grown in the Yemen. Mocha coffee, shipped exclusively out of the port to European markets, was favoured in the city coffee houses for its 'aromatic unique taste and therapeutic medicinal qualities'.

With the East Indiaman safely secured at anchor, Captain Pinnell was taken ashore on the ship's boat, to carry out the necessary transactions with the port authorities and Company agents. With the pig iron offloaded, sacks of coffee were ferried out by boat, hauled aboard, and stacked in the ship's hold, along with the remaining cargo and Company chests of treasure. The crews of East Indiamen were afforded leave to go ashore, to carry out their own trading privileges, although after many months at sea the men found the allure of beautiful, young, exotic, dark skinned women of North Africa and Asia too tempting to ignore, willingly using up their allocation of wages to partake in the delights on offer. These shore leave recreational activities resulted in many of the crew of merchant ships contracting and spreading venereal diseases, which manifested in the form of wounds and boils many weeks after the unfortunate mariner had left the port. The only remedy available to infected mariners was by the ship's surgeon administering mercury orally, or by painting the liquid onto the affected area of skin, remedies, which treated rather than cured, as sexually transmitted deceases were deadly and virtually incurable.

Once loaded with cargo, provisions and stores, the *Princess Louisa* left anchorage at Mocha in May 1734, sailing north-east out of the Gulf of Aden and into the Arabian Sea. After three months' sailing, the East Indiaman arrived at the British held Indian port of Bombay. The East India Company leased the port from the British government in 1668, for £10 per annum, when the port was not much more than a coastal fishing town. The Company transformed the natural deepwater harbour into an extremely successful trading port and Company stronghold, where migrants from all parts of India travelled to Bombay, taking advantage of the trading and employment opportunities available at the port. The migrants established small communities around the port and town that rapidly grew in size, their trading businesses and industries expanding to meet the demand of the goods much sought after in Britain and Europe. These goods, lightweight cotton cloth, silk, jewellery, herbs, sugar, spices, minerals, dyes, medicinal plants and western society's favourite social drink, tea, all brought vast profits for the Company and ship owner merchants. During the 1730s, the Company imported goods from the East Indies worth in excess of £2,000,000 annually. However, these trading opportunities were limited to the number of ships available to the Company for bringing in these goods from the East Indies and China and the Company began building East Indiamen in Bombay shipyards, employing local Indian craftsmen, using locally grown hard woods, which were superior to British oak and less susceptible to seaworm attack. With huge quantities of valuable cargo passing through the dangerous waters of the Arabian Sea and Indian Ocean, which included the chests of Company treasure, a great fleet of armed fighting vessels were built by the Company for the protection of the East Indiaman and the cargoes they carried. The fleet of fighting ships became known as the Bombay Marine and along with ships of the Royal Navy, they hunted down the pirates and privateers threatening Company interests.

The Company's increasing trading activities offered its employees lucrative working opportunities throughout the India subcontinent. These postings however, were believed to be extremely unhealthy for Europeans because of the hot and humid climate, where the average life expectancy of Company employees working in these conditions were considered to be only three years. Although there were many health issues faced by Company employees while living and working in India, those who braved the dangers to take on these posts were able to live an extremely comfortable lifestyle, with servants and slaves caring for their every need. Those who took passage to the East Indies were mostly young, single men, eager to make their fortunes. These young men were advised not to marry an English woman before they left, who in all probability would succumb to the climate and the heat, but to wait and take a local woman as a wife after they arrived. Nevertheless, it was not unusual for married Company employees to be accompanied by their wives when taking up these posts, resulting in an increase of the colonial population throughout British held territories in India. Between the time the East India Company took control of the port in 1668, to the day the *Princess Louisa* sailed into the harbour for the first time in 1734, the population of Bombay had increased from 10,000 to over 60,000 through migration and colonial occupation.

The development of the port of Bombay included the building of warehouses, a hospital, a harbour quay and a Company fort and mint, the destination of the thirty chests of Spanish silver aboard the *Princess Louisa*, off-loaded and brought ashore under armed-guard.

With transactions completed, provisions stored and the crew returning to the ship no doubt much the worse for wear from their exertions ashore, the East Indiaman was ready to make way, homeward bound. On leaving any port anchorage, fully laden sailing ships were required to manoeuvre away from the crowded harbour area and into a safe position of open water before raising sail. To do this the ship's crew were required to make use of a kedging anchor, to pull the vessel into a favourable position. A long rope attached to the kedging anchor was wound around the ship's capstan at the other end. The anchor was then rowed out as far as possible on the ship's boat and dropped down onto the seabed below, the crew aboard ship then turned the capstan to wind in the line pulling the ship towards the kedging anchor. This was an extremely long and time-consuming procedure, especially if the manoeuvre needed to be carried out on several occasions. On the day of departure, the *Princess Louisa* had been manoeuvred into position out in an open stretch of water away from the port's river traffic and was ready to make way under the captain's orders. However, tragedy almost struck as soon as the East Indiaman had raised anchor and lowered sail, the *Princess Louisa* was suddenly caught in an unexpected and extremely strong tide. With the weight of the cargo aboard the crew found it difficult to keep the East Indiaman on course taking the vessel safely down river. As Captain Pinell gave orders for the crew to adjust sail and the helmsman to bring the vessel around, the ship began to drift on the unpredicted tide. Lookouts cried out a warning that the ship was heading towards a reef showing just above the heavy swell. Captain Pinell immediately ordered the hands to drop anchor and lower sail to halt the ship's progression towards the jagged outcrop of rocks. The quick actions taken by the officers and crew undoubtedly saved the ship from near disaster where any collision with the reef would have torn out the ship's bottom planking, leaving the *Princess Louisa* wrecked before completing its maiden voyage.

East Indiamen were reliant on wind and tides before making way on long trading voyages, which meant ships could be waiting many weeks for favourable winds and sailing conditions before the ship would be able to set sail.

The *Princess Louisa* remained at anchor to await a more favourable tide, before she was ready to make sail once more, heading out into the Arabian Sea and onwards to the Dutch held port of Cochin on the south-west coast of India. From here, the East Indiaman sailed southwards to cross the Equator heading into the vast expanse of the Indian Ocean and then onwards towards the Cape of Good Hope arriving off the southern tip of Africa in December 1734. By January 1735, the East Indiaman had reached St Helena, a Company-held island off the west coast of Africa used as a welcome landfall by ships on route to and from the East Indies, Asia and China. The Company had taken possession of the island under a Charter issued by Charles II in 1659. The English East

India Company and Dutch East India Company, both fierce and competitive rivals, had fought over the island on several occasions; the English Company winning out in these skirmishes, ensuring St Helena remained under British rule. The island's inhabitants consisted of Company employees, English settlers and hundreds of slaves, who were used as labourers on the island, even after Britain had abolished the slave trade in 1807. The islanders traded and sold provisions and fresh water to ships making port at the island, where their crews carried out private trade with the islanders and the crews of other Company ships making port at St Helena.

The East India Company held island and port of St Helena, off the west coast of Africa – 1700.

The remainder of the *Princess Louisa*'s return voyage home was uneventful. Although occasionally encountering some heavy weather sailing northwards towards the Azores, the ship made good headway towards the English Channel, arriving off the Downs on 14 April 1735. The *Princess Louisa* completed its maiden voyage in just seventeen months, a relatively short voyage to the East Indies, which usually took an East Indiamen between eighteen months to two years to complete.

After a pilot had taken the *Princess Louisa* into the Thames, the East Indiamen proceeded up-river to Gravesend, where a Customs official came aboard and accompanied the ship further up river to moorings at Blackwall Reach. Captain Pinnell registered the East Indiaman's cargo at Customs House and the precious cargo of Mocha coffee was offloaded throughout the following week onto lighters that came up alongside the ship. Once aboard the lighters the cargo was then transported to the legal quays and loaded onto horse pulled carts, which were driven to warehouses in the city for storage and sale at market. During the early part of the eighteenth century, merchant ships returning from long voyages to the East Indies were required to offload cargoes at Blackwall Reach, after the river had become overcrowded with merchant ships and river craft. This had made it impossible for large merchant ships proceeding up-river to unload at quays and wharves at the centre of London. Due to the over congestion at the docks and quays, caused by the ever increasing amount of freight shipped into London, the cargoes of goods brought from the East indies could be left on lighters for weeks at a time, before they were able to be unloaded and despatched to the Company's warehouses in London's East End. These cargos were left on lighters and barges unprotected and vulnerable to theft by river pirates, where under the cover of darkness these armed gangs stole the goods off the barges under the noses of customs officials. Another trick of the river pirate was to cut loose a lighter from its moorings, which then floated down river on an outgoing

London's Legal Quays on the north-bank of the River Thames, between London Bridge and the Tower of London – 1746.

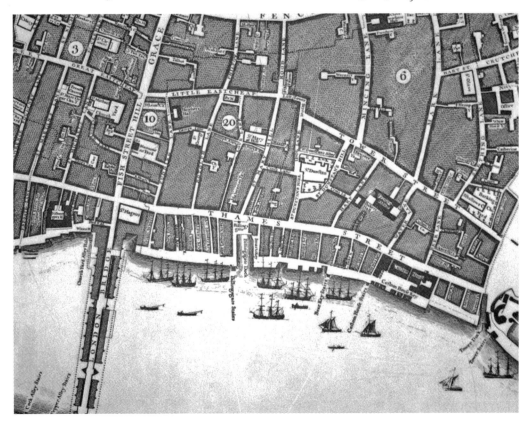

Imported cargo unloaded at London's Legal Quays off Thames Street, with the Tower of London in the distance – 1757.

tide where the lighter would then be retrieved downstream by the pirates with the cargo removed undetected. Hundreds of thousands of pounds were lost every year through the theft of goods by river pirates, an act that held harsh penalties for any river pirate caught and found guilty of the crime, resulting in the pirate receiving a sentence to hang by the neck on the gibbet on Execution Dock at Wapping. Once the pirate's life had been extinguished at the end of the rope, the lifeless corpse was taken downstream to Blackwall Point and hung in chains on Greenwich Marsh where the remains were left for all to see, serving as a warning to others intent on stealing goods brought in by East Indiamen moored opposite the gibbet at Blackwall Reach.

With the cargo of Mocha Coffee offloaded, the *Princess Louisa* returned to the dockyard for repair and refit which took just over eighteen months to complete. Towards the end of the summer in 1736, the East Indiaman had left the dockyard in preparation ready for its second voyage to the East Indies, bound for Calcutta. The ship's Husband, Thomas Hall, gave over the command of the ship once more to his good friend Captain Richard Pinnell.

The crew who signed on for this second voyage were a mixture of old hands, who had previously sailed on merchant ships bound for the East and West Indies, and a variety of inexperienced men and boys who had little prospects ashore and were hoping to make a living at sea. The ship's cargo for the outward-bound voyage consisted of 2,481 bars of pig iron, 1,268 copper plates, forty-four

anchors and a large quantity of leather hides, barrels of beer and
various wooden chests containing stationery and a variety of
medicines. Company officials also loaded aboard fifty wooden
chests each measuring three feet long, two feet deep and three feet
wide. Wrapped in sailcloth and bound with heavy rope, the chests
contained Company treasure worth in the region of £30,000.

The *Princess Louisa* left the Downs in November 1736, sailing
down the English Channel heading towards Plymouth Sound.
After dropping anchor and taking aboard more cargo and supplies,
the East Indiaman remained at anchor at Plymouth to await the
seasonal trade winds before proceeding southwards out into the
North Atlantic in January 1737. Making around seven to eight knots

*East Indiaman moored
off Blackwall with the
remains of a pirate
swinging on a gibbet
at Blackwall Point
– 1782.*

the East Indiaman sailed south-west past the Bay of Biscay and on
towards the Canaries, arriving off the Cape of Good Hope by mid-
March. Conditions throughout the first part of the voyage had been
favourable and the ship had been making excellent progress until
leaving the Cape behind when the weather suddenly changed for
the worse. Sailing on towards the Indian Ocean the *Princess Louisa*
sighted a vessel in obvious distress, with its masts and yards broken
and fallen away. The ship was the *Richmond*, an East Indiaman that
had been caught up in a violent storm on its return from China.
The *Richmond* had lost all top masts, the mainmast and main yard,
and the ship may well have been wrecked if the *Princess Louisa*
had not gone to the stricken vessel's aid. Captain Pinnell offered
the master of *Richmond*, Captain Gough, a spare topmast, spars and

rope to erect a jury rig, enabling the East Indiaman to make sail towards the safety of the nearest port to make repairs.

Back on course after the rescue of the *Richmond*, Captain Pinnell had to deal with a more unpleasant incident, which had taken place aboard the *Princess Louisa*. While on route from the Cape to Bengal, the ship's boswain, George Newman, was charged with committing sodomy against several members of the crew. Although this type of incident was not unusual amongst the crew of a merchantman, the act was a punishable crime, where if found guilty, the perpetrator faced a severe punishment which included a flogging, a forfeit of wages, or in some extreme cases, the penalty of death. Put into chains and placed in confinement, the boswain was left awaiting his fate until handed over to the Company authorities after the East Indiaman made port. A similar incident that took place on a Dutch East Indiaman resulted in the guilty party, Officer Leendert Hasenbosch, being set ashore and marooned on the uninhabited Ascension Island. In 1726, the crew from a British ship discovered his tent, clothes and a diary, but there was no sign of the officer himself.

The *Princess Louisa* arrived at the port of Madras on the east coast of India in June 1737. Portuguese traders had built the port after their arrival in the region during the early part of the sixteenth century. The East India Company purchased an area of land close to the port in 1639, where the region's ruler granted permission for the Company to build a factory, trading post and a warehouse. The following year the Company constructed Fort St George, the first British fort to be built in India. Goods loaded aboard Company ships at the port consisted of bales of cotton cloth, purchased cheaply in Calcutta then sold on at exceedingly high prices in London to supply the increasing demand in Britain and Europe for lightweight Indian cotton fabrics. On leaving Madras, the *Princess Louisa* sailed north, bound for Diamond Harbour and Rouges River, in the region of West Bengal. Diamond Harbour, once the stronghold of Portuguese pirates, was now used by East Indiamen laying up before proceeding onwards to Calcutta, the Company's furthest coastal outpost in India. Once free of the pirates who once terrorised the coastal waters of north-east India the region became an extremely important area for trade when the Emperor abolished all customs duties there in 1717. Free from these customs duties once paid on goods purchased in Bengal, traders and merchants took full advantage of the opportunity to acquire goods extremely cheaply and then sell them on at highly increased prices in England.

From Rouges River, the *Princess Louisa* sailed northwards into the Hooghly River estuary where pilot schooners were waiting ready to guide East Indiamen up river. There were many areas along the Hooghly River which were far too shallow for a fully laden ship to pass through and the river pilots who knew the hazards and dangers well, charged a fee to guide fully laden ships safely along the river, through deep-water channels to and from the anchorage off the inland port of Calcutta. The port had come under Company control when the Mughal Emperor transferred the rights of the local area over to the East India Company in 1698. At the port of Calcutta, the Company built a factory and the stronghold Fort William, to consolidate the Company's hold

The East India Company built Fort St George, Calcutta. Courtesy of Special Collections, University of Houston Libraries.

and domination over the region, which had became the centre of the opium trade under the control of the East India Company and the British Government. Positioned on the east bank of the Hooghly River, Calcutta, built on the profits made from opium, grew into the second most important city in the British Empire. Spreading out from the Company fort in the south to the powder mills towards the north, the city's expansion included the building of a government house and mint, wharfs and docks, a theatre, court house and a horse-racing track laid out to the south of a new Company fort which was built in 1781. With the *Princess Louisa* safely moored off the port of Calcutta, the outward-bound cargo was unloaded onto barges and the Company chests of treasure, drugs, stationary and beer were transported to the Company's factory and stronghold.

Spending many weeks on the Hooghly River, taking aboard cargo, provisions and stores, the *Princess Louisa* laid up at anchor on Rouges River, south of Calcutta for several weeks waiting for the seasonal trade winds to take the East Indiaman home. While the crew were kept busy carrying out maintenance, cleaning the ship and servicing the guns, suddenly, without warning the *Princess Louisa* was caught up in a great storm. Dense black clouds appeared in the sky and driving rain began to fall in torrents making it almost impossible to distinguish the river from the sky. As the ship rolled and strained upon its moorings under the gale force winds that swept along the river, pounding waves broke over the ship's forecastle sending water cascading down the forward deck. The force of the storm was so severe that the East Indiaman parted its cables and was set adrift on the river. Struggling to secure the ship's moorings, the crew lost the spare anchor overboard as the *Princess Louisa* was beaten about the river. The ship's main mast,

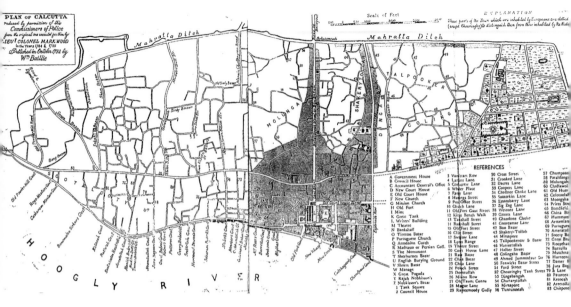

Map of the Port of Calcutta published in 1792.

damaged in the raging storm, was cut away, but plummeted down on top of the second mate and a crewman below, who were both killed instantly under weight of falling mast and rigging. The crew had no way of controlling the East Indiaman as the ship was driven by the wind and waves with great force, hard onto a sand bank, dislodging the longboat that was lost overboard. The East Indiaman began to fill with water through open ports, which the crew were unable to close when the storm hit and it seemed as if the ship would be totally wrecked. By morning although the ship had been blown off the sandbank the ship's hold was some four feet deep in water. As the storm eventually subsided, the crew were able to secure the ship's moorings as they began pumping out the waterlogged hold. Along with the damage sustained to the main mast and loss of the longboat, the ship's rudder had been badly twisted and bent out of shape. Captain Pinnell wrote in the ship's journal 'like storm has not been known in the memory of man'. With temporary repairs carried out, the *Princess Louisa* made for the Hijili tidal canal, around seventy miles south of Calcutta, before making sail for home.

In the spring of 1738, the *Princess Louisa* had reached the East India Company port of Jamestown on the island of St Helena to take on fresh water and provisions for the final stage of the voyage. The ship sailed north-west towards the Cape Verde Islands, then into the North Atlantic, heading north-east towards the English Channel.

On sighting Land's End, the *Princess Louisa* made its way up the English Channel passing Beachy Head on 7 August 1738, where the lookouts spotted the sails of three ships heading towards the East Indiaman. The three ships were British Royal Naval vessels *Elizabeth*, commanded by Captain Edward Falkingham, the *Augusta* and the *Dunkirk*. As the ships closed in on the *Princess Louisa*, the *Elizabeth* made a signal ordering the East Indiaman the heave to. A boat launched from the *Elizabeth* commanded by the ship's first lieutenant made its way across to *Princess Louisa*, where the naval party boarded the East Indiaman with the intention of pressing the ship's most experienced hands into the service of the Royal Navy.

On first sighting the Royal Navy ships, the crew of the East Indiaman had armed themselves with muskets from the ship's weapons store in expectation that the naval crew would try to board the East Indiaman in an attempt to impress members of the crew. In an effort to resist impressment the crew of the *Princess Louisa* banded together and a firefight took place between the crew of the East Indiaman and the naval boarding party. In a violent exchange of musket fire, able seaman Sam Robins was shot dead and fell overboard into the water.

After the loss of their crewmate, the men on the East Indiaman lost their enthusiasm for a fight and gave in to the naval boarding party, which resulted in several of the crew from the *Princess Louisa* taken for impressment into the service of the Royal Navy. The impressing of crew from British merchant ships was a legitimate and legal activity and although the Royal Navy were obliged to offer other men as replacements for the best of the men taken, these replacements were usually poor sailors who the navy no longer required. The impressing of merchant ships' crew at sea was extremely

common during the seventeenth to the eighteenth century, especially during times of war when the navy were in need of competent and experienced sailors. Captain Falkingham of the *Elizabeth* had been issued with specific orders from the Admiralty to sail to the Downs and intercept any merchant ships on a return voyage and to impress the men aboard. The officers and crew of any outward-bound merchant vessel were exempt from impressment, however they would not be so fortunate on the ship's return voyage home. Many merchant ships sailing into the English Channel would change course heading for Ireland at the first sight of Royal Navy ship, where the merchant ship's most experienced crew would then be put ashore in an attempt to save them from impressment into naval service. Captain Pinnell was powerless to intervene in the impressments of the most experienced members of the ship's crew and all that he was able to do was to make a report of the incident for the Company on the ship's return to port.

The Company and the East Indiaman's owners and shareholders may well have considered the death of any hands during a voyage and the impressment of crewmembers an acceptable loss, particularly when the ship's cargo brought such high rewards, which had been the case after the *Princess Louisa*'s second voyage to the East Indies, which had been an extremely profitable one. After the rigours of the second voyage, where the ship had suffered damage in the storm on Rouges River, the East Indiaman returned to dock in September 1738 for repairs and refit, which would take just under eighteen months to complete.

For the ship's third voyage to the East Indies the *Princess Louisa* would be sailing under a new commander, Captain John Pinson, a very capable and experienced merchant ship officer.

With Britain's continued conflict with Spain developing into a declaration of war on 23 October 1739, the *Princess Louisa's* voyage to the East Indies could prove to be an extremely dangerous and hazardous one. British merchant ships sailing to the East Indies were liable to come under attack not only from pirates but now from Spanish privateers, well armed and well-manned private ships given licence by the Spanish government to cause havoc and mayhem for any British ship found on the high seas. As a majority of the Royal Navy ships were stationed off the south coast of England, in expectation of France entering the war on the side of Spain, merchant ships had some protection while sailing down the Channel towards the Atlantic. However once out into open waters, East Indiamen were liable to come under attack once reaching the Spanish privateer cruising grounds off the Spanish mainland and the North African coast. When the *Princess Louisa* sailed for the East Indies in April 1740, holds loaded with a cargo and the Company's chest of treasure securely stowed below, the crew were constantly on the lookout for any sign of a sail which could potentially be a Spanish privateer, with a the *Princess Louisa* a prime target for attack. Sailing south then westwards as far away as possible from the Spanish cruising grounds, the East Indiaman sailed safely through the North Atlantic making a course towards the Cape of Good Hope. From the Cape, the *Princess Louisa* sailed north-west into the Indian Ocean towards Madras, the ship's first scheduled port of call arriving in August 1741. Once the cargo had been off-loaded, the East Indiaman first sailed to Calcutta before cruising the Indian Ocean over the following five months, sailing and trading from port to port, loading and off-loading cargos of saltpetre, redwood, guns and pepper. Although the ship had kept clear of any confrontations with privateers and pirates, the voyage did not go without loss of life, as several of the East Indiaman's crew died after falling from the rigging when the ship encountered storms and rough weather conditions while sailing throughout the Indian Ocean.

When the time came for the *Princess Louisa* to return home, the East Indiaman first headed for port of Tellicherry on the Malabar Coast, arriving on 5 February 1741, to load aboard 600 sacks of Tellicherry peppercorns, considered the finest pepper in the known world commanding exceedingly high prices on the British spice market. While sailing at sea for many weeks at a time, the news of any developing conflict between Britain and Spain would be extremely difficult to obtain. The crew on the East Indiaman continued to be wary of sighting a sail on the horizon, especially if the ship was flying the French flag, as it would not have been known if the French had made any alliance with the Spanish during the time the *Princess Louisa* had been at sea. Furthermore the French held territories on the Indian coast of Malabar and had been in constant conflict with the Dutch and the English over trading rights in India since the late seventeenth century and East Indiamen were wary of sailing too close to the coast in fear of coming under attack by French privateers. On leaving Tellicherry the *Princess Louisa* kept well clear of the Malabar Coast, heading towards the Cape, from where the ship sailed north-east on to St Helena, arriving off the island in May

1741.

On leaving St Helena behind the *Princess Louisa* sailed north towards the Cape Verde Islands, staying westwards of Spanish-held waters around the north-west coast of Africa. On 8 September, a lookout aboard the East Indiaman spotted a sail on the horizon, but was unable to make out the ship's nationality. The following day the same ship was sighted in the distance making the same course as the *Princess Louisa*, the unidentified ship then hoisted the red, white and blue French tricolore. With Captain Pinson unsure whether the French had joined the Spanish in the war against Britain, or if the ship was in fact a Spanish warship masquerading as a Frenchman – tactics which Spanish ships had used during the war – he kept his ship at a safe distance. On 10 September, the French ship had been joined by several other vessels and the crew of the East Indiaman were worked hard to keep the *Princess Louisa* well ahead of French ships. The following day the ships were nowhere to be seen, however they re-appeared two days later shadowing the *Princess Louisa* as she was making a course towards the English Channel. Making good headway and excellent speed, the *Princess Louisa* left the French behind and by 23 September, the East Indiaman had made it safely to the Downs after a third successful voyage to the East Indies.

After just over a year in dock for repairs and refit, the *Princess Louisa* was ready for charter once more by the East India Company. The Company and owners had every faith in the ship, its master Captain John Pinson and the quality of hands signed on for the ship's fourth voyage. The East Indiaman's Husband Thomas Hall considered the *Princess Louisa* to be an extremely fine and sturdy

The dockyards at Deptford at the turn of the seventeenth century, with ships under construction and repair on the slips, with several warships and merchantman anchored off Greenwich Reach.

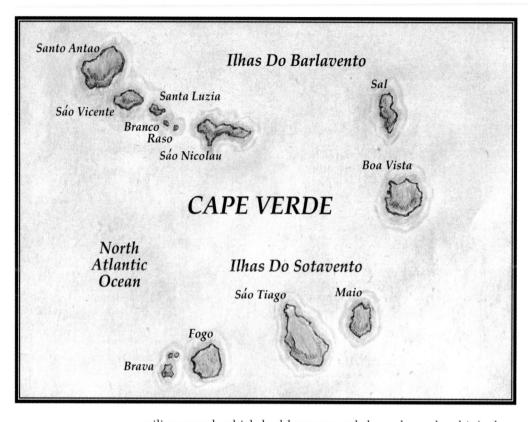

Santo Antao

Ilhas Do Barlavento

Sal

Santa Luzia

São Vicente

Branco
Raso

São Nicolau

Boa Vista

CAPE VERDE

North
Atlantic
Ocean

Ilhas Do Sotavento

São Tiago   Maio

Fogo

Brava

The Cape Verde Islands were a notorious area for wreckings, where archive documentation records there may be as many as 300 shipwrecks spread out throughout the group of islands off the North West coast of Africa.

sailing vessel, which had been proved throughout the ship's three previous voyages. When the East Indiaman sailed on 4 March 1743, bound first for Bandar-Abbas in Persia and then on to Bombay, the East Indiaman's owners and shareholders had every expectation that the *Princess Louisa* would make another successful and profitable voyage to the East Indies. The ship's complement totalled 116 men captain, officers, crew and a company of soldiers. The ship's hold was fully loaded with bails of woollen cloth and textiles for trading in Persia, with guns, gunpowder, sailcloth and cordage bound for the Company factories in the Far East. Included within the cargo, were over 800 ivory elephant tusks and twenty chests of Company treasure, each chest filled with over 200 lb of Spanish-American and Spanish silver reales. The return cargo would include bails of silks and cotton textiles, and large quantities of spices and dyes. The *Princess Louisa* sailed from Portsmouth, accompanied by the East Indiaman *Winchester*, and a convoy of smaller merchant vessels under escort from the *Stirling Castle*, a Royal Naval seventy-gun third-rate ship of the line.

Once clear of any waters where the convoy may have come under attack from privateers, with Britain still in conflict with Spain, the *Princess Louisa* and the *Winchester* sailed away from the convoy, heading towards the Cape Verde Islands off the west coast of Africa. The group of small islands, which were first colonised by Portuguese traders, were located in a prominent position on the shipping lanes between Africa, America, Europe and the Far East, making the islands the perfect location for trading ships to take on fresh water and supplies, as well as carrying out private trade with the colonists. The Cape Verde Islands became an important location in the Trans-Atlantic slave trade where the islands' prosperity attracted the unwanted attention of pirates, who regularly attacked the capital Ribeira Grande, which had once been sacked by the English privateer Sir Francis Drake. The natural harbour of Mindelo, on the island of Sao Vicente, developed into an important commercial centre and port of call for visiting merchant ships of all nations.

Fully laden with cargo, both ships were making good headway south towards the islands, with the *Princess Louisa* sailing ahead of the *Winchester*. A lookout on the *Princess Louisa* spotted Boa Vista, the furthest island east of the group on 17 April 1743. Captain Pinson gave orders for the ship to head towards the group of islands, with the *Winchester* following on the same course, approximately a mile behind. A further day's sailing brought both ships in close towards the islands, where each vessel shortened sail ready to navigate through the islands' hazardous waters. As darkness began to close in, the lookouts on the *Winchester* could clearly make out the stern lights of the *Princess Louisa* as the vessel sailed on ahead.

The captain of the *Princess Louisa* had no orders to make a call at the island, as the Company's business was in Persia and Bombay and after only four weeks of sailing, neither ship was required to take on any further provisions or supplies. The course the *Princess Louisa* was heading seemed to be taking the East Indiaman towards the island of Santiago, the largest and most important island in the group. Merchant ship captains often carried more cargo aboard than was officially recorded on the ship's manifest during outward-bound voyages, for conducting private trading transactions on route to the East Indies. Any private cargo carried by the East Indiaman would in all probability have overloaded the ship, which increased the draft by around six feet. However, any private trade the captain of the *Princess Louisa* may have been intending to carry out at the Cape Verde Islands would go unrewarded, as sailing close to the wind and forging ahead of the *Winchester*, Captain Pinson had set the East Indiaman on a course that would lead the ship towards disaster.

At midnight, the small island of Maio was sighted south-east of the *Princess Louisa*'s position east of the main island of Santiago. After sailing on for just over an hour, with the *Winchester* following on the same course as the *Princess Louisa*, on a heading taking both ships northwards around the island of Maio, the crew aboard the *Winchester* were startled to hear the boom of a gun echoing out across the water.

Off the north shore of the island of Maio, a submerged peninsula known as Galleons Reef stretched out from the shore seawards, covering some seven square miles of open water. Any ship sailing across these shallows would undoubtedly meet with disaster on the submerged rocks, especially if the ship was overloaded with cargo and lying too low in the water. As the *Princess Louisa* came around to the north of Maio, the crew on watch spotted the white tops of waves breaking across the reef and realised the East Indiaman was heading directly towards the dangerous shallows. The order was given to fire the ship's gun to signal a warning to the *Winchester* that the ships were heading into a perilous situation. On hearing gunfire, the crew of the *Winchester* quickly changed course, away from the *Princess Louisa*'s position and away from the shallows. As the *Winchester* sailed on, the crew watched in horror through the fading light, as the *Princess Louisa* sailed directly into the waters breaking over the rocks of Galleons Reef.

It was now much too late for the *Princess Louisa* to change course away from the reef and the East Indiaman struck the submerged rocks hard several times. At 1.30 a.m. on 19 April 1743, the East Indiaman became stuck fast on the jagged rocks, causing severe damage to the ship's hull below the waterline. The crew began to jettison the ship's guns overboard in an attempt to refloat ship, a futile act that made no difference to the plight of the vessel. The crew were left helpless as the waves breaking across the reef battered forcefully into the ship and across the deck, washing away anything that was not tied down. Throughout the night, the waves continued to break over the ship rolling the vessel further onto the reef, where the continued onslaught of water eventually brought down the East Indiaman's masts and rigging. At daybreak two boats were launched from the *Winchester* in an attempt to get close to the *Princess Louisa* and take off the crew who were standing upon the deck waving and calling for rescue, however the seas were far too rough and the boats had to pull away to save themselves from being wrecked upon the reef. The surge of waves began to swamp the stricken ship, tearing away at its upper structure, causing sections of the ship to break off and fall crashing into the sea. Although the ship's hull had remained intact during the night by 9.00 a.m. the next morning the hull had broken in two, sending the ship's cargo spilling out across the reef and into the sea. The captain of the *Winchester* attempted another unsuccessful rescue and unable to see any of the *Princess Louisa*'s crew alive on deck the captain of the *Winchester* presumed that all the crew had been lost and ordered the ship's boats to be raised before setting a course away from the *Princess Louisa* leaving the stricken vessel to its fate.

Aboard the *Princess Louisa*, a majority of the crew were still alive and when they realised that any attempt of rescue by the *Winchesters* boats would be impossible, Captain Pinson ordered the crew to abandon ship. The East Indiaman's captain, senior officers and a number of able seamen and soldiers, had no option than to take their chances and jump down into the sea, making for landfall. The remainder of the crew, numbering some seventy men, opened up the ship's brandy and drunk themselves into a stupor in the ship's forecastle, giving up all hope of rescue.

The men who had jumped off the ship to take their chances in the sea, suffered severe cuts and gashes scrambling through the waters and rocks of reef attempting to make their way to the safety of the shore. Those who managed to secure belongings and valuables before leaving the ship were then stripped of all their possessions by

East India House, Leadenhall Street, London. Erected in 1762 to replace the original timber built Company offices.

the islanders including the clothes they were wearing, before the Portuguese authorities were able to come to their rescue.

The survivors were taken by boat to the Island of Santiago, east of Maio, and after recovering from their ordeal, arrangements were made for their return, first taking passage to the Caribbean and America, before joining ships heading for England. Captain Pinson, several officers and remaining crew, were taken aboard the Royal Naval sloop *Hound*, on route to Virginia, from where they later found passage home to England. William Gordon, Captain of the *Hound*, reported the loss of the *Princess Louisa* in despatches sent to the Admiralty where he recorded the loss of life as seventy-four, with survivors numbering forty-two.

It would be several months before Captain Pinson returned home to face a board of enquiry and investigation into the loss of the *Princess Louisa*. At the East India Company headquarters in Leadenhall Street, London, Captain Pinson and the surviving officers were found not guilty of negligence for the loss of the ship, where the cause of the wrecking was recorded as the result of inaccurate charts and unknown currents.

The East India Company, the ship's husband Thomas Hall and the ship's shareholder owners, decided that it would be financially beneficial to attempt to salvage whatever was left of the Company cargo, specifically the twenty chests of treasure containing almost two tons of silver reales. The exact location of the wreck was never plotted and all of the ship's papers, which may have given the Company a clue to where the wreck lay, had been lost. Even so, a contract was drawn up between the parties to form a private syndicate to send an expedition to attempt to find the lost treasure of the *Princess Louisa*. Two ships were fitted out and heavily armed for the salvage operation; the first of two expeditions began in 1744. All attempts to locate any of the *Princess Louisa*'s precious cargo were unsuccessful and the second salvage attempt ended in failure, resulting in the loss of one the syndicate's ships captured by the French while returning to England. No trace of the ship could be found, the remains washed away by the waves breaking across the reef. The cargo of ivory tusks, canons and iron and lead ballast, along with the Company chests of treasure were scattered about the reef and rocks and down upon the seabed where the *Princess Louisa* had broken up after the wrecking. This magnificent ship, built at Deptford Dockyard, once the pride of the East India Company, had met a similar fate as many other merchant ships, which had fallen foul of the extreme forces of nature encountered while sailing the trade routes around the globe.

The Princess Louisa's
final destination
Galleons Reef off the
island of Maio.

A new age of sail - the clipper *Hallowe'en*

The clipper ship Hallowe'en *sailing through the East China Sea – 1874.*

A large expanse of Greenwich Marsh, situated between the dockyard sites of Deptford and Woolwich, had up until the early 1800s, only been fit for the grazing of cattle and at its furthest point north, the hanging up of river pirates in chains. When both the Royal Dockyards closed in 1869, shipbuilding on the Southbank of the Thames almost came to a close, all apart from one shipyard on Greenwich Marsh, which kept these traditions going, building and launching iron boats and ships at Bay Wharf. The first building to be erected on the Marsh was a large government gunpowder

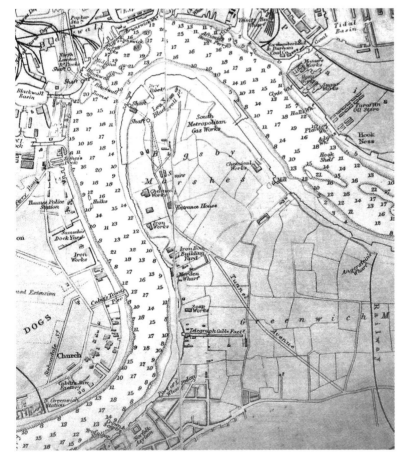

Greenwich Marsh late 1800s, with a dry dock to the north and the Iron Boat Building Yard located upon the western shore at Bay Wharf.

magazine built in 1694, used for the storage and testing of this dangerous and volatile material. It was not surprising that area remained under-populated for many years, due to the potential risk of explosions. Towards the end of the 1700s, the magazine was sold and the Marsh was gradually taken over by riverside yards, building boats, barges and later ships made of iron. Much of the area towards the centre of the Marsh was taken up by commercial industries producing and manufacturing steam engines, chemicals, building aggregates and marine telegraph cables.

A majority of Greenwich Marsh came under the ownership of Morden College, a charity founded by Sir John Morden in 1695, a rich city merchant and board member of the East India Company. The charity was formed for the benefit of fellow merchants who had fallen on hard times when losing their estates and livelihood, after the ships and goods they had invested in were lost through the dangers and perils of trading at sea. The charity was funded by donations made by wealthy city merchants and investments made in purchasing property and land, such as Greenwich Marsh, leased out to make huge profits which would be invested back into the charity. The ships owned by these city merchants, sailing under charter of the extremely powerful and influential East India Company, were built at the dockyards of Deptford and opposite Greenwich Marsh at Blackwall.

Towards the end of the 1700s, the British Government was become increasingly concerned about the amount of power and control the Company held throughout the East Indies and by the mid-1800s, through legislation and acts of reform, the British Government nationalised the Company which eventually lead to the loss of all its administrative powers and possessions in India. Once the trading monopoly with India had been broken, the Company was dependent on financial income made from ongoing trade with China and concessions allowing the Company to continue importing tea from India.

Many East Indiamen, under charter to the Company, were now transporting cargoes of tea from both India and China. The lack of any serious competition in the tea trade meant that there was no reason to improve the sailing qualities of these vessels, resulting in voyages continuing to be slow taking some eighteen months or more to complete. These voyages could take even longer during severe seasonal tropical weather conditions and storms, when East Indiamen captains would rather lower sail until the weather improved, rather than take the risk of sailing through it. This resulted in the cargo arriving in poor condition, stale and suffering from water damage after long voyages. Even though the imported tea sold at market was of a poor quality, the shipments continued to make the Company shareholders, merchant traders and ship owners extremely wealthy, no matter how long shipments took to arrive from the Far East, as the imported tea had become an expensive luxury commodity.

After Britain's triumph at the Battle of Trafalgar in 1805, Britain's domination over the seas and oceans of the world continued throughout the remaining years of sail. Not only was this down to the superiority of the Royal Navy's fighting fleets, but also because of British economic ascendancy around the globe. This in turn made trading voyages around the world much safer than ever before. With the restrictions imposed on the East India Company's trading activities in the Far East and with trading voyages less likely to come under attack from rival trading nations, large armed merchant ships – which had become costly and uneconomic to build and maintain – were no longer financially viable. As there was now less need to heavily arm East Indiaman, the design and shape of the merchant ships

began to change, taking into consideration the distribution of weight above the waterline, when heavy guns were no longer required. The double raised poop deck and galleries found on earlier merchant ships were also lowered resulting in a reduction of weight aft of the ship, which contributed the to an increase in speed under sail. Although the shipping lanes had become much safer for merchant ships to cruise on trading voyages to the Far East, pirates and privateers continued to operate off the coasts of the most remote regions around the world. This resulted in the building of the Blackwall Frigate in 1830; an East Indiamen designed and built to resemble heavily armed single decked naval frigates, which a pirate or privateer would have second thoughts about attacking.

Blackwall shipbuilding yards to the right with several trading ships off-loading cargo into Thames lighters and skiffs moored at Blackwall Reach, mid-1700s.

The first of these new East Indiamen was built across the Thames opposite Greenwich Marsh, in the yards at Blackwall, from where these frigates acquired the name. The term Blackwall Frigate would eventually be used to describe all these new type of East Indiamen, whether built in other British yards or in the yards of India.

At one time all imports of tea into Britain had been paid for in silver, then as the value of silver increased, the Company offset the total cost of the tea by paying a third of the price in opium, a drug originally used for medicinal purposes to assist sleep, redress stress and deaden pain, however opium was also taken for the pleasurable experiences it gave the user. China imported a majority of the opium which was grown and produced in India, however due to the drug's addictive properties the taking of opium for recreational use was banned by the Chinese government in 1729.

Opium Clipper from the mid-1800s, the designs upon which tea clipper evolved.

A trade dispute between Britain and China over the importation of opium resulted in hostilities breaking out between the two nations known as the 'Opium Wars', which the British eventually won, gaining control over the opium trade in 1860 and the British colony of Hong Kong in the process. The trading of opium became big business for the East India Company and was fully supported by the British Government. Although Company ships were forbidden to carry the drug aboard, the Company managed to get around this problem by using independent traders to smuggle opium into China. The fast sailing vessels manned by these smugglers were top-sail schooners and were known in the trade as 'opium clippers'. These swift craft were smaller than the Blackwall Frigates, however, they carried more sail in relation to the size of the vessel's hull. Many of these clippers were built in Scottish shipyards and were designed and constructed to sail in the worst of weathers and through the tropical monsoons, carrying opium from the Indian ports of Bombay and Calcutta into the Chinese ports of Shanghai and Hong Kong.

Last days of an East Indiaman, dismantled and moored up in the Thames Estuary. (William Adolphus Knell, 1850)

Although opium was shipped legally into Britain, for medication and recreational use, the biggest profits continued to come through the importation of tea. The time taken for ships returning with precious cargoes of tea, was dictated by seasonal weather conditions and the tea growing seasons in India and China. The first ship to return to home port with the freshest cargo of tea was assured of the biggest rewards, bringing further financial benefits for the Company, merchants and ship owners, along with extra bonuses for the ship's crew.

During the early 1800s the East India Company's trading monopoly had been worth almost £30,000,000 a year, however by 1878 the Company, which had been managing Britain's tea interests on behalf of the government, was effectively dissolved by Acts of Parliament which opened up the tea trade to independent traders. Although the Blackwell frigates continued to sail to the Far East under private trading charters, merchants needed even faster ships to bring home the highly prized shipments of tea from the Far East. With the tea trade now open to all, the American merchant ship owners were the first to begin building a new type of merchant sailing vessel based along the lines of the opium clippers. These new merchant ships were designed specifically for the tea trade,

The Black Ball Line clipper Ocean Chief *during an Australian run, with the crew aloft on the yards reducing sail. (Attributed to Samuel Walters, 1853)*

73

Small river craft plying their trade off Greenwich Hospital during the 1800s. Many of these types of vessels were built on Greenwich Marsh during 200 years of the areas boatbuilding and shipbuilding history.

many sacrificing cargo capacity for speed. The clipper had a sharper prow and a distinctively wider bow, allowing the ship to move more swiftly through the water, and carried much more sail to make good use of the seasonal trade winds. Although Blackwall Frigates continued to sail the trade routes to India and China, a majority now only carried passengers rather than cargo and the clipper ship began dominating the sailing trade routes around the world. The technological advancements being made in steam-powered ocean going vessels during the mid-1800s, may have been considered a threat against ships powered by wind and sails, however steam ships were still unable to match a clipper for speed and financial efficiency until the beginning of the twentieth century.

Opposite the shipyards at Blackwall, the yards on Greenwich Marsh were kept busy constructing all types and sizes of wooden and iron river craft, which included fishing boats, lighters, skiffs and Thames Sailing Barges, which worked the river between the eighteenth and twentieth centuries. The Thames Barge evolved from lighter barges used to transport goods and cargoes from ship to shore, first built of wood and later in iron, there were over 2,000 sailing barges working on the Thames and the coastal waters of Kent and Essex throughout this period of time.

In 1864, an American boat builder from New York leased an area of riverside land on the Marsh known as Bay Wharf, from Morden College, the bay had been used as a slip for small boat and barge building since the early 1700s. Also known as Horseshoe Breach, the bay was formed by a break in the sea wall which had left a small open inlet on the west of the Marsh. The American boat builder and marine engineer, Nathan Thompson, designed and developed a system of building identical river craft on a production line, which cut down on manpower and production time, making the iron boats extremely economical to produce.

Thompson's production line boat building system was designed to use steam powered machinery which required a large financial investment from his company backers. The company prospectus contained letters of recommendations from the Duke of Cambridge, Duke of Sutherland and many other well known established shipbuilders and industrialists, including MP Colonel Sykes, Chairman of the East India Company. Thompson's company, the National Company for Boat Building by Machinery, intended to produce up to 6,000 small boats each year and with the boat builders' investments in place, the development of Bay Wharf began. A boom was put into place across the entrance of the bay, a causeway was built and the river wall was refaced with stone. New modern brick-built workshops were erected on the site to accommodate the steam-powered machinery which would be used to produce the iron boats on an assembly line. For a year the boatyard successfully manufactured the iron-built boats as expected, all to a standard size and produced in volume on a production line, the company nevertheless failed to sell all the boats they had made, and Thompson's boatbuilding company soon went out of business. However the financial investment made at the site, ensured that Bay Wharf would continue to build iron boats and ships for the next forty years.

Marine engineers, Maudslay, Sons & Field, took on the site, with the intention of constructing iron-built steamships. The company founder, Henry Maudslay, born in Woolwich, learned his trade working under Marc Brunel, father of Isambard Kingdom Brunel. The company's origins were in the design, development and production of industrial and marine steam engines, built at its works in Lambeth, South London. After Henry Maudslay's death his sons, Thomas and Joseph, decided to expand the family business into shipbuilding. The yard on Greenwich Marsh was the ideal location where the engineering company would be able to design, build and launch iron steam ships.

The first ship launched at the yard in 1865 was the 576 ton, iron-built steam collier *Lady Derby*, named after the wife of Prime Minister John Russell. Even though steam powered vessels were considered to be the future of the merchant shipping industry, sailing ships still held huge advantages over steam powered ships, especially when encountering storms and extreme weather conditions where heavy seas washing over a steam ship's deck and finding its way down into the engine room, would easily extinguish the steam boilers. Sailing vessels were also more economical to operate, required less crew to man them and continued to be faster than steam ships on long voyages where steam powered vessels were required to carry large loads of coal to power the ship's engines and then make port more often during the voyage to take on extra loads of fuel.

With the decline and fall of the East India Company, independent merchants and traders began building fleets of merchant ships for trading between Asia, the Far East, Australia and America. One of these independent merchant ship owners was the Scotsman, John Willis, the eldest child born into a family of mariners at

Above: *John 'White Hat' Willis, ship-owner and mercantile merchant trader. 1817 – 1899.*

Right: *Square rig clipper* Tweed, *converted from a paddle steamer of the Bombay Marine.*

Eyemouth, north of Berwick-on-Tweed. John Wallis's father had learned his trade as an apprentice on an East Indiaman after having an argument with his step father and then running away to sea. The young Scotsman then went to work on a coaster, where he rose through the ranks from an able seaman to ship's master and later in his seafaring career he became an extremely successful ship owner and businessman. At the beginning of the nineteenth century, merchant ship owners were divided by class, from former shareholders and ship's husbands of the East India Company, down to merchant ship captains who bought a ship with their saved earnings, gradually building up a small fleet of ships from the profits earned through their trading activities. John Willis was one of these ship owner traders, who brought his family into the shipping business. He appointed his eldest son, John, as master of a succession of the family's merchant ships, where three of his five younger sons were also involved in working at sea. After the family moved from Scotland to Wapping, in the East End of London, two of John Willis's three daughters married into a Scottish family of Marine Chandlers, John Kirkaldy & Son, who were also based in the East End of London.

On the death of John Willis senior in 1862, his eldest son took over the family business, John Willis & Son Ship Owners and Brokers. John Willis moved the family home from Wapping to a large private residence, Cardigan House, in Richmond Surrey, where he lived with his widowed mother, his youngest brother, unmarried sister and his nephew, the son of a brother lost at sea.

In that same year John Willis & Son purchased two former East India Company ships for £44,000, the *Assaye* and *Punjaub*, former armed paddle steamers of the Bombay Marine built in yards at Bombay. John Willis then sold the *Assaye* for £40,000 and converted the *Punjaub* into a sailing vessel, selling its two steam engines for £12,000, where the funds raised were used to pay for the vessel's conversion. The sailing ship was renamed the *Tweed* after a river on the Scottish borders close to where the Willis family had originated. John Willis had become a popular figure in the world of merchant shipping, earning the nickname 'White Hat' through his habit of never going ashore unless wearing his customary white top hat. His shipping business had also become very well regarded within maritime circles and apprenticeships with John Willis & Son were extremely sought-after positions, where young men could earn from around £5 for the first year, up to £10 in their fourth and final year as an apprentice.

An iron ship under construction on the slips during the early 1800s, built using the latest engineering technologies, which were at first not always successful.

By the mid-1800s, independent ship owners were commissioning fast new clipper ships to be built to meet the demands of the increasing India and China tea trade industry. Before the conversion of the *Tweed*, John Willis had commissioned the building of the company's first full rigged composite clipper at yards in Rotherhithe, a few miles along the river west of Greenwich. This new clipper was launched in 1862 and was name *Whiteadder*, after a tributary river of the Tweed.

The very first of the clippers had all been constructed in wood, with the first iron clippers built from the 1820s onwards. These iron-built ships had many advantages over timber-built vessels, which included savings in construction costs, an increase in storage capacity and hull strength. The iron-built hull was able to withstand greater stresses than timber-built ships. However the disadvantages of the iron-built ships came through in their performance, when the hull below the waterline became covered in weed and barnacles during long voyages in the tropics, which caused an increase in drag through the water, reducing the ship's speed, manoeuvrability and sailing qualities. Iron ships could not be sheathed in copper as corrosion occurred when copper and iron came into contact in salt water. There was also a problem with corrosion in the ship's bilge when salt water settled in the cargo space, which in turn resulted in the cargo becoming contaminated through poor ventilation. These problems were eventually resolved by laying cement in the bilge and adding ventilation shafts in the ship's hold.

With both types of clipper construction having its advantages and disadvantages, the ideal solution was to combine the materials and build composite ships, where timber would be fixed over the vessel's iron frame and then the hull could be sheathed in copper below the waterline. The iron frame giving the ship improved strength without sacrificing speed and sailing quality.

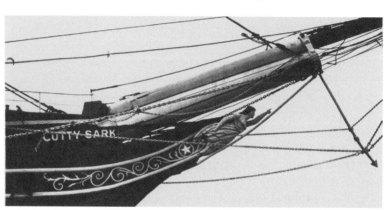

Above: *The ship* Cutty Sark *at sail on the open sea during one of the clipper's early trading voyages.*

Right: *The original* Cutty Sark *figure head 'Nannie' the witch made famous through the poem 'Tam O' Shanter' by Robert Burns.*

Both the converted *Tweed* and the composite-built clipper *Whiteadder* proved to be extremely good sailing ships, bringing John Willis a healthy profit from his company's tea trade ventures. Following on from the success both these ships brought John Willis, the ship owner commissioned a further three new clippers for his fleet. The first would be designed and built at the Dumbarton firm of Scott & Linton. Hercules Linton, a partner in the firm, drew up the designs for the clipper, incorporating the *Tweed*'s bowlines into the drawings to create an innovative hull shape for this new composite-built vessel. Before the ship was completed Scott & Linton had found themselves in financial difficulties, which forced the company into bankruptcy, with the clipper left high and dry on the stocks. After negotiations took place between the yard owners William Denny & Brothers and the ship owner John Willis, they came to an agreement where the owners of the yard would complete the building of the ship. On 22 November 1869, the new clipper was launched into the river Clyde and christened the *Cutty Sark*. Although undoubtedly a beautifully designed ship,

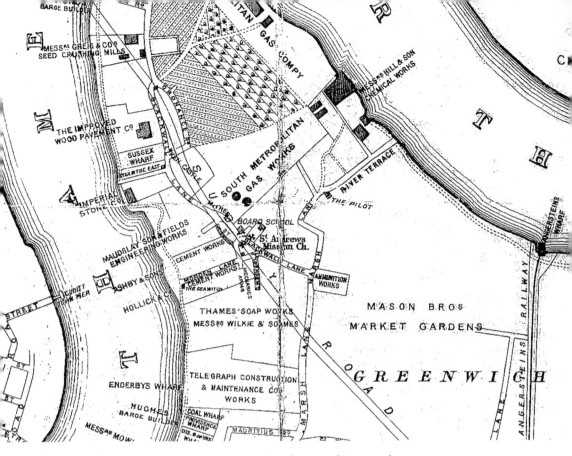

The following text labels appear on the map:

BARGE BUILDER
MESSRS GREIG & COS SEED CRUSHING MILLS
THE IMPROVED WOOD PAVEMENT CO
SUSSEX WHARF
STAR THE EAST
IMPERIAL STONE CO
MAUDSLAY SON & FIELDS ENGINEERING WORKS
CEMENT WORKS
ASHBY & SON
CUBITT PIER
HOLLICK & CO
THE SEAWITCH
BORDEN LANE CEMENT WORKS
MECHANICS ARMS
BOARD SCHOOL
St Andrews Mission Ch.
WALL LANE
AMMUNITION WORKS
STREET
THAMES SOAP WORKS
MESSRS WILKIE & SOAMES
MASON BROS
MARKET GARDENS
GREENWICH
ENDERBYS WHARF
TELEGRAPH CONSTRUCTION & MAINTENANCE CO WORKS
HUGHES BARGE BUILDER
MESSRS MOW.
PROVIDENCE WHARF
COAL WHARF
MAURITIUS
MARSH LANE
ROAD
RAILWAY
ANGERSTEINS LANE
MESSRS HILL & SON CHEMICAL WORKS
RIVER TERRACE
THE PILOT
SOUTH METROPOLITAN GAS WORKS
METROPOLITAN GAS COMPY
GERSTEINS WHARF

which would later prove to also have superb sailing qualities, at the time of its launch the *Cutty Sark* was just one of many fast clippers sailing the seas and oceans of the world during the late nineteenth century.

John Willis, an old sailing hand himself, continued to favour sailing ships over steam powered vessels, which were costly to build and uneconomical to run and there were many other merchants and ship owners who shared these views, believing that sail power would remain superior to steam power for many years to come. When John Willis first commissioned the building of the *Cutty Sark,* construction had just begun on the Suez Canal, which would open up a waterway between the Mediterranean Sea and the Red Sea, reducing the distance steam ships were required to travel from Western Europe to the Far East by some 4,000 miles. The expected outcome was that sailing ships would no longer be able to compete against steamships as they were unable to navigate the canal under sail and would have to continue to sail around the Cape of Good Hope, which would inevitably bring an end to the tea trade for sailing clippers. In spite of this John Willis continued with his plans to have two further clippers built, designed along the same lines as

The site of Maudslay, Sons & Field's Engineering Works during the early 1900s, located towards centre left of the map.

the *Cutty Sark.* However as a businessman first he was reluctant to invest a large sum in the building of these two ships, if indeed it did come to pass that steam was soon to take over from sail, deciding to have the clippers built as economically as possible.

Both ships were going to be constructed in iron, more cost effective and quicker to build than timber or composite built vessels and the company of Maudslay, Sons & Field won the contract after putting forward a very low estimate to obtain the work. Both of these ships, built on the company's slips at Bay

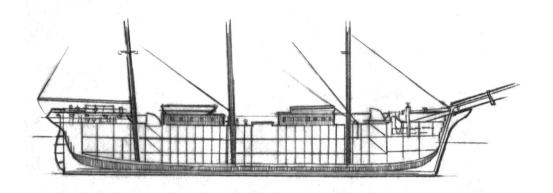

Both new iron clippers built for John 'White Hat' Willis were designed along the lines of the composite built Cutty Sark.

Wharf, were the only clippers ever to be built on Greenwich Marsh.

Traditionalist shipbuilders were reluctant to take on the building of iron ships, preferring to continue using tried and tested methods and materials in wooden ship's construction. The building of iron ships required new ideas in ship design and construction, which traditional shipbuilders were not suited to, so the craft of iron shipbuilding was developed by mechanical engineers, which Maudslay's, innovators in the design and development of machine engineering, intended to bring into iron shipbuilding. The plans of the two clippers were based upon those of the *Cutty Sark,* with each measuring 216.6 feet in length, with a beam of 35.2 feet and a depth of 20.5 feet. Both of the clippers would be registered at just over 900 tonnes when completed.

With designs of the ship and the plans drawn up, the yard's workshops began on the fabrication of the ironwork used in the construction of both clippers. The yard's crew first laid out the ship's keel, made up from sectional plates riveted together. From the keel the ship's ribs, girders made up from plates of iron, were riveted into place each side of the keel. The ship's stem bar, a continuation of the iron keel, was set out to be much sharper than the stem bar on a wooden-built ship.

The outer hull was made up from sheets of iron-plating, around an inch thick, cut to shape using huge steam powered shears and then shaped to fit using steam powered pressing machinery. The plates were then punched through with holes ready for riveting into place on the iron ribs of the vessel. The ribs were tied together and held in place by beams of iron, which also supported the ship's decks. The beams were bound together at their outer ends by stringer plates and longitudinal and diagonal tie plates, which were then covered by wooden lengths of deck planking. Watertight iron plate bulkheads were built into the clipper's bow and stern and the

Blackadder *under sail after several faults had been rectified during the ship's construction.*

ship's raised forecastle was built up to take the windlass, used for raising the anchor and cable chain. On completion of the hull, the clipper was ready for fitting out after launch.

On 1 February 1870, the first of the two Maudslay-built clippers was launched from the company's slipway and christened the *Blackadder*, named after a tributary of the River Tweed. All of John Willis's ships were given names which had connections with Scotland, or places close to the family's ancestral home near to the borders. The celebration by the yard's crew and engineers at the *Blackadder*'s launch was as much in relief as it was in delight at the successful launching. Although both clippers were designed and built to the specifications and requirements laid down by Lloyds of London, Maudslay, Sons & Field were not experts in large ship construction and they had underestimated the costs in building the clippers to secure the contract, the largest the yard had taken on. The latest technology and machinery used by Maudslay's in iron shipbuilding were still in the experimental stages and the construction of these two big sailing clippers came through trial and error, once afloat ready for fitting out, faults were found within the *Blackadder's* construction which had to be rectified before the clipper could be completed. The ship's bowsprits, yards and booms were also made from iron-plate, formed into half tubular shapes

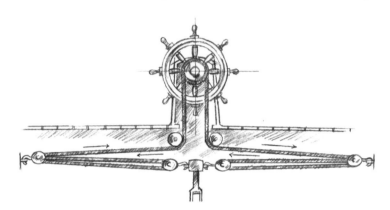

A clipper ship's steering gear, operated by the ship's wheel, where the rudder would be moved to port or starboard by a cable wound around a revolving drum and pulleys and then attached to the tiller.

then riveted together to make hollow tubes. Each of the clipper's upper masts were made to slide into the lower masts, methods first used in the construction of iron steamships and composite built clippers. The steering gear on this iron-built clipper would be comparable to the gear used on earlier built clippers, which consisted of a vertical spoke wheel positioned on the poop deck, working a revolving drum, the cable and pulley connected to a short iron tiller, with the gear supported by a heavy iron-built frame. The rudder was made up from sectional iron frames with iron plates riveted into place each side.

The main mast of both clippers each measured just over 150 feet in height. The use of iron masts and iron wire rigging, if fitted correctly, added extra integral strength, however in some iron-built ships, the masts had collapsed due to poor riveting and insufficient internal strengthening. In just under a month after launch and with the faults found during fitting out believed to have been made good, the *Blackadder* was ready for sea, bound for Shanghai on its maiden voyage to the Far East on 24 March 1870, a voyage which almost became a complete disaster.

While the clipper's sister ship was still under construction on the slips at Maudslay's yards, the *Blackadder was* sailing on a course heading towards the Cape of Good Hope on the southern tip of Africa. By May 1870, the *Blackadder* had been making good headway towards the Cape, when unexpectedly the clipper's mainmast and mizzenmast collapsed mid-Atlantic. The clipper's crew erected a jury rig, a temporary replacement mast and yards, which enabled the stricken vessel to limp into the port at Cape Town, despite colliding with two other vessels when entering the harbour. With the *Blackadder* forced to make repairs at the Cape, Maudslay, Sons & Field continued on the building of its sister ship unaware the *Blackadder* had been dismasted.

John Willis & Son Company flag, flown from mainmast of the company's fleet of merchant ships.

By early summer 1870 the clipper on the slips at Maudslay's yard was ready for launch, which received a great amount of publicity and local interest, especially as news had reached home of the disaster which had beset the *Blackadder*'s maiden voyage. With the John Willis company house flag flying high from a flagstaff on the clipper's deck and a bottle of port suspended from the bow ready for breaking to christen the ship, the crowds gathered along the foreshore of the shipyard getting ready for the celebrations to begin. John Willis, members of his family, Maudslay's officials, the yards crew and the workshops engineers and machinists, all waited in anticipation for the call 'down dogshores', the signal to knock out the last of the holding blocks. When the shout went out gentlemen's top hats and the yard workers' caps were raised and tossed into the air and the crowd cheered and applauded as the clipper slid slowly down the slipway towards the Thames. The bottle of port was broken across the vessel's bow as the ship entered the water on 4 June 1870, and the clipper was then christened the *Hallowe'en*.

Deck of the Cutty Sark *looking forward, both* Blackadder *and* Hallowe'en *were similarly rigged however the masts of the* Hallowe'en *were set out in such a way that more air was able to fill the upper sails between forward and main masts, making the ship extremely swift in light airs.*

The fitting out of the clipper began soon after the launch and a majority of the *Hallowe'en*'s fixtures and fittings were made off-site, from the brass port lights to the ship's longboat. Ships' chandlers, John Kirkaldy & Son, through the family connections with John Willis, supplied a majority of the materials, fittings and equipment for his company ships and carried out most of their fitting out and maintenance, keeping the work within in the family businesses.

After the disastrous maiden voyage of the *Blackadder*, when the masts had collapsed, Maudslay's needed to ensure the same would not happen to *Hallowe'en*; in all probability, the collapse was due to the poor riveting of the masts and insufficient internal stiffening, which caused them to come down. The *Hallowe'en*'s masts, however, were securely fitted in place and were set slightly raked like those of a Chinese Junk. The foremast was raked slightly forward, the mainmast upright and the mizenmast raked slightly aft. Clipper designers at the time were of the opinion that clippers'

The Hallowe'en *moored at the quayside in the course of a tea run to China during the late 1800s.*

masts should be raked less and set up similar to the masts on the *Cutty Sark*, however the way the masts had been set on up on the *Hallowe'en* would later prove to be of the clipper's advantage. In the early nineteenth century, clippers' masts were divided into three sections, lower, top and topgallants, each mast carrying three square sails, with the top masts carrying an extremely large sail on the fore and main masts. This sail needed to be furled by men climbing out on the yards to complete the task by hand when the sail was not required, a task which was extremely time consuming and hard to carry out when the ship was tossing and rolling in heavy seas. The sail configuration on clippers continued to evolve throughout the late 1800s and these large sails were later divided into an upper and lower sail for ease of use and practicality. When running under full sail each of the clipper's three masts, the fore, main and mizzen, carried six square sails. Triangular stay sails were carried between the fore and main masts and the main and mizzen masts. Towards the stern of the clipper a large spanker was carried aft of the mizzen mast. The bowsprit, forward, carried a triangular jib and four stay sails running to the fore mast. A fully rigged ship carried a set of forty-six sails, with each one individually made and stitched together from lengths of flax canvas. Each clipper usually carried two sets of sails during a voyage, one set well used for fair weather sailing and the newest set brought out for heavy weather conditions.

The captain's quarters, officer's cabins and pantry, along with the officer's saloon were all built into the poop house towards the stern of the ship. The captain's quarters consisted of a cabin with large bunk, sideboard and wardrobe and a day room fitted out with a table, sofa, bookcase, chart racks and instrument cupboard. The captain also had the luxury of his own toilet and metal bath. The remainder of the officers' cabins each had a small bunk, a sofa with draws fitted below, a sideboard, bookcase and a table with a hinged flap containing a metal washbasin. The clipper's saloon was well equipped with a small iron stove, a custom built wooden table and set of chairs, fitted shelving along the walls and built in sideboard and cupboard for storing bottles and glasses. The boswain, carpenter, cook, sailmaker and ship's apprentices were accommodated in a cabin-house built up on the deck between the main mast and foremast, which also included the carpenter's workshop and the galley. The remainder of the crew were berthed in cabins forward on the lower deck. All the crew, captain, officers, able and ordinary seamen and apprentices now slept in fitted bunks, as hammocks were no longer used on merchant ships. The officers' quarters, saloon and crew's cabins were fitted out in stained and painted wooden tongue and groove paneling. The ship's storage area and vast hold, which carried around 1,500 tons of cargo, were located on two decks below the clipper's weather deck, taking up virtually all of the space within the clipper's hull.

The problems which Maudslay, Sons & Field had discovered during the fitting out of the *Blackadder* and the subsequent collapse of the masts, had brought about lawsuits between the owner and the builder, resulting in the *Hallowe'en* not being handed over to John Willis until almost eighteen months after the clipper's launch. On the return of the *Blackadder* in November 1871, the ship's underwriters had refused to pay out in full for the damage the ship sustained during the voyage, which resulted in John Willis vowing never to take out insurance on any of his ships ever again.

The *Hallowe'en* was ready to go to sea in the spring of 1872, however by the time the lawsuits had been settled, it was far too late in the season for the clipper to sail for China to take on a cargo of tea. Three of the company's ships the *Tweed, Blackadder* and *Cutty Sark*, had already sailed for the Far East and John Willis, quick to look for other profitable trading opportunities rather than just depending on the tea trade, made the decision to send the *Hallowe'en* south to Australia, where the clipper was to take on a cargo of wool.

When appointing a ship's master, John Willis not only relied on the captain's experience and quality of his seamanship, he also depended on the financial success which the captain would bring to the company. The masters of clippers, much like the masters of an East Indiaman, had the opportunity to supplement their pay by conducting their own business activities during the voyage and although John Willis gave his masters a free hand in these trading activities he never offered them any interest in the ships, which was customary at the time. A clipper's master received a high level of social standing, especially if achieving fast, record breaking voyages, reports of which were printed in all the local and national newspapers. These sailing exploits captured the imagination of the public to such an extent that they would follow their favourite ship's progress around the globe. Telegrams were sent by cable giving the ship's latest position as the clipper arrived at some distant port or sailed past many land based lookout points on route, the ship's position would be reported in the shipping news pages of the national broadsheets of the day. Large sums of money were waged on which ship would return from the Far East before any others, which brought the winning ship and master welcome notoriety as well as financial bonuses and rewards for completing fast, successful and profitable voyages. A first-class clipper captain could earn around £200 a year plus bonuses, although the adulation, fame and fortune which came to the ship and its master, did not always find its way down to the lower ranks, where in pursuit of celebrity and wealth, the captain would often work the crew extremely hard and exceedingly harshly for very little pay. Many clippers, along with the crew, were often driven to destruction in the search for speed in an attempt to earn the ship's owners, captain and officers, extra profit and increasing prosperity, where daring decisions made by the clipper's master, could bring either rich rewards or disastrous consequences.

The man appointed as master of the *Hallowe'en* on its maiden voyage was Captain James Watt, an experienced merchant mariner with plenty of sailing years behind him. The remainder of the ship's complement, officers and crew, came from various social classes and many nationalities. With the crew berthed, kit stowed, stores and provisions taken aboard, the clipper was towed downstream from Greenhithe on 12 June 1872. As evening approached, the *Hallowe'en* was secured for the night at a buoy off the Kent riverside town of Gravesend. Even though the clipper had been made fast, the ship drifted on the current during the night, colliding bow first with a ship moored close by. On inspection the clipper showed no sign of damage and at daybreak the *Hallowe'en* continued on its journey downriver, however at 9.00 a.m. the carpenter reported the ship was taking on water forward and even though the pumps were working to full capacity, the level of water had not reduced. The *Hallowe'en* was then towed slowly back to Gravesend with the pumps working full out and a telegram was immediately sent to John Willis to inform him of the situation. After his arrival later that day to inspect the ship himself, he ordered the *Hallowe'en* back to the South West dock for urgent repairs.

A week later, once the repairs had been made, the clipper continued to take on a small amount of water at the bow, but it was not enough to discourage Captain Watt from giving orders that the *Hallowe'en* was ready to make way. The clipper's boatswain and twelve of the crew confronted the captain and refused to sail, claiming that the ship was unsafe. The ship's master did not take this insubordination lightly and he immediately discharged the rebellious crew members from their duties. After the ship arrived at Gravesend, a replacement crew was searched out and then signed on, with a full complement of men now aboard, the *Hallowe'en* finally took to sea on its maiden voyage.

The crew of the *Hallowe'en* included the captain, the first and second mate, a carpenter, sailmaker, steward, cook, boatswain, sixteen able seamen and one ordinary seaman. The crew came from all parts of the world, England, Scotland,

Ireland, America, Finland, Germany and Prussia. All but one, the able seaman, were experienced hands who would have encountered their fair share of harsh and dangerous sailing conditions while serving at sea, however a serious situation arose between the captain and crew which almost broke out into open mutiny before the clipper left home waters. On 25 June 1872, with the *Hallowe'en* sailing down the English Channel towards Land's End, the clipper

INWARD.						
A LIST of the Crew and Passengers arrived in the Ship *Hallowe'en* of *London* to *Sydney* New South Wales, 18 *Sept* 1872.						*James Watt* Master,
of the Burthen of 920 Tons, from the Port of *London*						
SEAMEN'S NAMES.	Station.	Age.	Of What Nation.	NAMES OF PASSENGERS.	Description.	Remarks.
W. Greatrex	1 Mate	33	Eton			
James Carter	2nd do	23	Aberdeen			
Alexr Milne	Carpenter	46				
Henry Foster	Sailmaker	33	London			
Alfonzo Taylor	Steward	23	Ipswich			
James Austin Hill	Cook	39	Boston			
John Blair	AB	21	Dundee			
Thomas E. Blaine	AB	42	London			
William Davis	AB	20	Teignmouth			
Thomas Wilson	AB	40	Belfast			
Arthur Lane	Ud	17	London			
Thomas Wright	AB	26	Malton			
Thomas Thomas	AB	23	S. Shields			
Henry Robinson	AB	22	Fork			
Hendrick Holm	AB	27	Ireland			
Charles Heintzabel	AB	24	Germany			
Thomas Hanaway	AB	23	Pool			
William McDonald	Boatswain	39	Dundee			
John Kruger	AB	24	Prussia			
John W. Gibson	AB	56	Rochester			
John Jonson	AB	22	Finland			
Karl Holmgren	AB	22				
John Bonner	AB	27				
Francis Boyack	AB	21				

encountered some extreme heavy weather conditions. Pitching heavily in the large rolling waves, the clipper began taking on water forward where the crew, apart from the boatswain and two able seamen, confronted Captain Watt, refusing to carry out their duties in the fear that the ship was sinking. Captain Watt tried to reason with the men, making it clear he would not pull back and he would do whatever was necessary to ensure the safety of the ship, 'as if defending my own life'. The men continued to protest and refused orders to continue in their duties, telling their captain they did not want to continue on the voyage. Captain Watt then

Crew list from the first voyage of the Hallowe'en *after the clipper's arrival in Sydney during 1872, to take on a load of Australian wool.*

The Hallowe'en *anchored in Sydney Harbour late 1800s.*

threatened to lock them up without provisions, which was an idle threat, as in reality the clipper's master needed these men to sail the ship. Reluctantly, Captain Watt promised the men that if they continued with the voyage they would not be prosecuted after arrival in Sydney, for refusing to carry out their expected duty. The idea of possible prosecution seemed to persuade the rebellious crew members to reconsider their stance, and the crew returned to their duties under some protest, carrying out running repairs while under sail.

Sailing through the heavy weather, the clipper crossed the equator heading southwards and on towards Sydney, arriving after only sixty-nine days sailing, a remarkable time for the clipper's first voyage, especially considering the problems the clipper had first encountered. There was no doubt that the *Hallowe'en* was an extremely fast sailing ship.

The *Hallowe'en* came to anchor in Sydney Harbour off Port Jackson in September 1872, ready to off-load its outward bound cargo. The harbour port of Sydney on the south-east coast of Australia had first been colonised by the British eight years after Captain Cook had landed at Botany Bay in 1770. The British Government instructed Commodore Arthur Phillip to sail to these new lands and establish a penal colony at Cook's landing place of Botany Bay. On arrival Commodore Phillip considered Botany Bay to be unsuitable for occupation and sailed further northwards along the coast. His fleet of ships came across a large natural harbour which Captain Cook had marked on his charts, and which Commodore Phillip named Sydney Cove after the British Home Secretary at the time, Thomas Townsend, 1st Viscount Sydney. The harbour and the surrounding area was home to an estimated population of around 6,000 Aborigines when Commodore Phillip had first arrived. A year later a French expedition which sailed into the harbour was thought to have been responsible for the spreading of smallpox throughout these Aboriginal clans, which killed them in their thousands. As British convicts and colonists continued to arrive those Aborigines who had survived the disease were driven out from the region through colonial expansion and exploitation. By the early 1800s it was estimated that there were less than 300 Aborigines still living on their ancestral lands around Sydney harbour.

Once the clipper was safely moored, a majority of time in harbour was taken up with unloading and loading the ship's holds, carried out with great skill and care by the local stevedores. After first discharging the cargo and ballast from the ship after arrival, the crew were then required to clean out and fumigate the hold, before the stevedores loaded the ship with the next cargo, ensuring every space in the hold was not wasted. After completion of their duties the crew had an opportunity to go ashore, to relieve the pressures and rigours of their voyage. Most of the crew would spend their time and wages on drink and women. When their funds ran out and pleasures came to an end, their options would be to return to the ship or seek their fortune elsewhere, which often resulted in countless crewmembers of clippers jumping ship, especially during the Australian gold rush of 1851. However there were always plenty of men to be found at distant ports down on their luck, willing to work for a passage home.

The crew of clippers making port in Sydney were made most welcome by the colonials, where there was always plenty of hospitality available, with many young girls ready to take a walk out with clipper apprentices during their time ashore, before departing the port and heading for home, as this verse from an old wool clipper sea shanty aptly describes:-

Short term romances were a way of life for young men away at sea for many months at a time, where sailors really did have a girl in every port.

Fare you well, you Sydney girls, time for us to go!
The Peter's at the fore truck, and five thousand bales below,
We've a dozen shellbacks forrard, and a skipper hard as nails,
And we're bound for old England and the January Sales!

The 'dozen shellbacks' referred to in the shanty were members of a clipper ship's crew who had crossed the equator during their time at sea. With the *Hallowe'en*'s own 'shellbacks' ready to make sail after the cargo had been stowed aboard, which consisted of leather hides, barrels of oil, copper ore, bales of cotton and over a 1,000 tons of Australian wool packed in large bales. In the early 1870s, over seventy percent of Australian wool trade was handled through British merchants, where a shipment of wool consisting of around 5,000 bales, would be valued at around £100,000. On leaving port the *Hallowe'en* sailed eastward, south of New Zealand, running within the ice zone to take advantage of the strong westerly winds. On the constant lookout for icebergs, the clipper rounded the dangerous waters of Cape Horn before making a heading northward, through the Atlantic and onwards into the English Channel. The cargo aboard the *Hallowe'en*, when sold after the clipper's return home, made John Willis a very large profit from his initial outlay and although the ship's first wool run had been a financial success, the *Hallowe'en*'s fame would come through sailing voyages made on the tea trade routes to China.

Many clipper ship owners were indifferent to incidents occurring aboard ship involving captain, officers and crew during a voyage and as long as the vessel reached its destination and then returned safely with goods intact, clipper masters were left to get on with running a ship as they saw fit. Following the *Hallowe'en*'s financially successful voyage to Australia, which at first had not gone without a fair share of difficulties at the outset, Captain Watt was once again appointed master of the clipper for a second voyage, sailing to Shanghai to take on its first cargo of tea. Signing on new crew, including four apprentices the youngest just fourteen years old, the clipper's outgoing cargo consisted of fifty tons of beer, 1,240 tons of assorted merchandise and fifty-four tons of various commercial liquids. With crew mustered aboard and berths allocated, a tug towed the *Hallowe'en* down river and the clipper was ready to make sail in March 1873, heading first to Sydney and then on to China.

After only a month out at sea, the *Hallowe'en*, while racing with another clipper the *Leander*, was caught up in a violent south-easterly squall, which tore away the vessel's bowsprit, top mast and main top gallant. The crew took in canvas and proceeded to carry out running repairs, rather than make port and lose valuable sailing time. When the clipper's masts and rigging were later found washed up ashore, and with no sightings of the clipper having been made or any notice of the clipper making port for repairs, it was assumed that the clipper had in all probability been lost with all hands. There was great relief for all concerned, when the news arrived in London that the *Hallowe'en* had arrived safely at Sydney in June 1873.

This arduous voyage was too much for the clipper's boatswain, Henry Gainer, who immediately jumped ship on arrival at port, followed closely by the cook and then the ship's steward, Alexander Lonamore, who the captain was glad to see the back off, as the man had been drunk on several occasions while on duty during the voyage. Crew desertions on long and dangerous sea voyages were common, as life aboard a clipper was extremely hard and physically exhausting. The ship's crew worked in two watches, four hours on and four hours off, with all hands on deck when the ship encountered heavy weather. In violent storms the clipper's crew frequently risked their lives on deck, where large waves beating over the ship could wash a man overboard in an instant. Those working high up on the yards and spars faced the possibility of falling to their deaths, or plummeting into the waters below with no hope of rescue if they lost balance or their grip as the ship was tossed about in a storm. One crewmember needed to be at the wheel of the ship at all times and in heavy weather and rough seas, two men were needed to hold the ship on course, facing the danger of being washed overboard, unless they lashed themselves down.

The life of a merchant sailor brought many dangers, where the harsh and hostile conditions at sea saw many crew lost through shipwrecking, falling from rigging or contracting an incurable disease.

When the clipper was sailing in fair weather the crew were kept busy washing the decks, cleaning the ship and carrying out routine maintenance and repairs. Clippers sailed at the best possible speed in all weathers and sea conditions faced throughout a voyage, where the crew were continuously hard pressed to get the best out of the ship at all times. Clippers' masters were often considered no better than slave drivers, dealing out severe punishments to any member of the ship's crew who did not perform their duties as required. The *Hallowe'en* was an extremely fast and a good sailor in light airs, however the clipper would become difficult to handle when hard pressed in big seas, where the quarterdeck would be awash if the clipper was not quickly relieved of its aft canvas. The ship's master was dependant on the obedience of his crew, who were all required to carry out his orders precisely, otherwise they could all find themselves wrecked along with the ship.

After the cargo of the *Hallowe'en* was off-loaded at Sydney, the clipper took on 1,300 tons of coal bound for Shanghai, where there was an ever growing demand for this fuel. With the crew aboard, including the replacements for the three men who jumped ship, the clipper set course for China. Finding fair weather conditions throughout the voyage into the North Pacific, the clipper sailed into the China Sea towards the end of August arriving at Shanghai on 13 September 1873.

The port of Shanghai, once a small fishing town on China's east coast, had grown into an important trading port and gateway to inland China. During the mid-nineteenth century, at the conclusion of the opium wars, Shanghai was opened up to international traders through the Treaty of Nanking signed between the British Government and the Qing Dynasty. The colonial powers of Britain, America and France established their own territorial settlements within Shanghai, which were gradually populated by colonists from these trading nations. The sprawling town was criss-crossed with narrow roads and alleyways, each lined with small wooden and brick-built terraced houses and shops, festooned in brightly coloured hanging signs and banners. The rows of crudely built market stalls, situated along the roadsides and in market squares, offered all types of exotic goods and wares for sale from cheap oriental charms and trinkets to expensive silks and spices. The Nanjing Road, running east to west through the town's centre,

One of the many Chinese opium dens of the late nineteenth century supplied with drugs through the British importation into mainland China.

became a major area for the importation of foreign goods through British held concessions and was the first international shopping street in Shanghai.

To the east of the town centre, facing onto the mouth of the mighty Yangtze River, a much darker side of Shanghai could be found, where down gloomy lanes and passageways a sailor would be able to seek out a gambling parlor, brothel, tattoo salon, or opium den, where after many weeks at sea they would spend most, if not all of their hard earned allocation of pay, before returning to the ship much the worse for wear from their over indulgences and with their pockets empty. The opium trade was a huge international industry throughout the nineteenth century, where shipments of the drug were imported from British held Indian poppy farms and processing works to Shanghai and through into mainland China. The British defended their rights to trade in opium claiming the Chinese would only deal in this commodity to balance out the payments made to them in silver, to purchase tea for exportation.

When the *Hallowe'en* was exporting tea out of China during the 1870s, opium accounted for almost half of China's total imports.

Once clippers had discharged their outward bound cargoes, the ship's commander, either under instruction from the ship owner's agent or under his own initiative searched out a charter for a cargo of tea for shipping back to England. However they were not always successful in obtaining a charter for tea and would often have to resort to sailing between ports to find any type of cargo, rice, oil, coal or timber, which the clipper shipped throughout the Pacific Ocean and China Seas until the seasonal crops of tea came down river on boats from the plantations in the provinces to the port of Shanghai.

When a tea crop eventually arrived at the port, frantic activities followed as negotiations took place between clipper captains, agents and merchants to secure the highest charter for a cargo of tea, the best price at the time came to around £4 a ton. The tea, contained in large wooden chests, would be loaded aboard the clipper and stowed in the holds by Chinese labourers, experts in packing the chests tightly into every available space. So valuable was a cargo of tea, that the chests and boxes would be stored in the officer's and crew's quarters, under bunks, in lockers, any space which was readily available. Once fully loaded the clipper would sail almost immediately, with the captain using all of his experience and knowledge of winds and tides to make the fastest passage home, bringing the season's first shipment of tea back to market before any of his rivals. London society's affluent tea drinkers believed that the freshest crop of tea made the best drinking beverage, ensuring

Cargoes of tea aboard a clipper were stored in wooden chests in the hold and any other space which could be found aboard ship. Each shipment would bring huge profits for the merchants and bonuses for the clipper's crew.

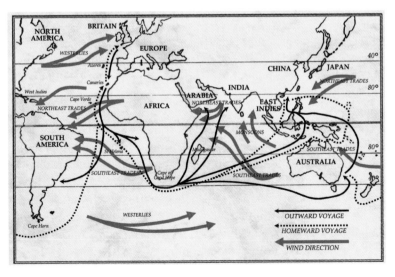

The wind patterns around the globe were the sailing ships' great source of power. These revolving masses of air created the Trade Winds which carried merchant vessels east and west around the oceans of the world.

93

that the first tea shipment to arrive from the Far East brought the clipper owner the largest profits. Two months after arriving at Shanghai the *Hallowe'en* had successfully secured its first shipment of tea, consisting of 5,500 chests, 11,075 half chest, and 2,917 boxes, the cargo also included 955 boxes of wax and 62 packages of hats. Accompanied by the customary striking of ship's bells, firing of

Battling against the elements to bring a cargo of tea safely home, the Cutty Sark *is caught up in a typhoon off the Formosa coast in 1873.*

signal guns and cheering from the crews on clippers at anchor, the *Hallowe'en* made way out of Shanghai on 17 November 1873.

Captains of merchant ships sailing out of the East Indies, Asia and the Far East had several courses to take in bringing the cargo home in the fastest possible time, which would be dependant on the seasonal wind and weather conditions in both Northern and Southern Hemispheres. Experienced and daring clipper ship captains would sail the most direct course whatever the season. On leaving Shanghai the clipper sailed with the prevailing north-east trade winds into the South China Sea, sailing down the east coast of China to take advantage of the land breezes coming off shore which assisted in taking the ship south. The clipper would then make a heading towards the Philippines and the Greater Sunda

Islands of Borneo, Java and Sumatra. Once through and clear of the narrow Sunda Strait, the clipper sailed into the Indian Ocean. An inexperienced or less daring clipper ship master may have preferred to take a much safer route by first sailing eastwards towards the Pacific then south east of the Philippines making for the island of Timor, from there the clipper sailed westwards into the Indian Ocean, a much slower course to take especially if carrying the season's first cargo of tea, where the highest profits made on shipments relied on the swiftness of the clipper's return. Once into the Indian Ocean the clipper made a course heading south-west for the Cape of Good Hope, using the south-east trade winds to take the ship into the South Atlantic. On occasion a sailing ship may have been caught up in the Doldrums, an area of sea along the equator where the north-east and south-west winds converged and the high temperatures cause the winds to rise upwards, leaving ships becalmed in the water. However Captain Watt had no problems with the weather on the return voyage home, where the clipper's master took full advantage of the available trade winds to bring the *Hallowe'en* home in just ninety-two days sailing, an extraordinary time for the clipper's first return voyage from China. The year before the *Thermopylae* had made a run of 122 days in a race with the *Cutty Sark* which had lost its rudder sailing through the Sunda Strait, arriving a week later. The *Hallowe'en* had beaten the sailing time of the *Thermopylae* by thirty days and the Greenwich-built

Left: *Surviving dockside warehouses at West India Quay on the Isle of Dogs.*

Below: *Thames waterman's skiff boat loaded with stores for merchant ships moored up in London's docklands.*

clipper would better this time the following season.

At the end of the return voyage the *Hallowe'en* was taken under tow into the Thames Estuary and upstream to the London docks to discharge the cargo of tea for carriage to the warehouses. The huge dock complexes were built at the beginning of the nineteenth century on land both north and south of the Thames to accommodate the increasing numbers of merchant ships brining in goods from all parts of the world. The proposals for the development of the docks were resisted for many years, especially by Thames watermen and lightermen, where for over a hundred years they had earned a living moving cargoes from ships to warehouses and wharfs all along the river. With the building of the docks their livelihoods were threatened when ships were now able to discharge goods directly from ship to shore. To lessen these concerns and to ensure that the docks would not hold a monopoly over the handling and storage of goods, the Government passed an Act to allow lighters and barges free access to the docks where they were able to carry out their trade of moving ships' cargoes for storage to cheaper warehousing along the river.

The clipper's next voyage under the command of Captain Watt took the ship first to Sydney then on to Shanghai to secure the season's first shipment of tea. For an iron-built clipper, the *Hallowe'en* was an exceptionally swift sailing vessel and had evidently made a name for itself after the previous season's remarkably fast run home, securing a charter of tea with considerable ease after arrival in Shanghai. On the 21 October 1874, the *Hallowe'en* sailed out of Shanghai arriving home, holds packed with chests of tea, by January 1875 after a record ninety-one days, a remarkable sailing time for an iron-built clipper. Captain Watt remained with the *Hallowe'en* for another season before a new master was appointed by John Willis, an audacious Scotsman Captain John Warrender Fowler, who had first gone to sea when just a boy and worked his way up to become a ship's master by his mid-twenties.

Master of the Hallowe'en, Captain John Warrender Fowler, one of the clipper's most experienced and successful commanders sailing the tea trade routes to China.

After the opening of the Suez Canal, steam ships were becoming more economically viable in carrying cargoes of tea through the canal. Although clippers were still comparatively quicker than steam ships, the clipper needed to sail the furthest course around the Cape of Good Hope. Towards the late 1800s, the tea clippers had been forced to look for other cargoes in other parts of the world, with many taking to the Australian wool trade, including the *Cutty Sark*. The *Hallowe'en* however did not follow this trend and persevered in shipping tea from China, which the clipper was exceptionally good at. Under the command of Captain Fowler, the *Hallowe'en* continued making excellent runs home from China rivalling the runs made by many of the more famous clippers of the time.

During voyages made by the ships in John Willis's merchant

fleet, there were many occasions when there was a need to transfer crew between vessels. One incident occurred during a voyage in June 1880, when the *Hallowe'en*'s first mate, William Bruce, was transferred to take command of the *Cutty Sark*. While the *Cutty Sark* had been sailing from Sydney to China, transporting a cargo of coal, an extremely unpleasant episode took place aboard the ship which resulted in the master of the clipper taking his own life. The *Cutty Sark*'s first mate, Sidney Smith, who it seems was a bully disliked by most of the crew aboard, killed able seaman John Francis, one of three black sailors who had joined the crew in Wales when the ship was loading a cargo of coal. The crew had no liking for these three black sailors, no doubt in those times because of the colour of their skin. The first mate taking an instant dislike to Francis, who he considered a clumsy and incapable seaman, made life a misery for him aboard, treating him extremely callously throughout the voyage, which escalated into a fist fight between the two men. Later when the crewman injured his hand in a bunting block while shifting the mainsail, the first mate began cursing and swearing at Francis for his ineptness. In obvious pain, the crewman immediately let out a tirade of abuse aimed at the first mate and both men once again began trading blows. The crew where now on the side of Francis as chaos erupted on deck. Captain Wallace broke out the small arms to attempt to restore order, demanding Francis apologise to the first mate which enraged Francis even more and both the men continued throwing punches at each other. The captain allowed them to fight on, threatening to shoot any man who interfered. Eventually however, with neither man willing to give way, Captain Wallace brought an end to the affair and cautioned the ship's crew that he would put any man in irons who abused his officers again. Nevertheless this was not the end of the matter, when the clipper was making a course towards the Sunda Straight, Francis was given an order by the first mate that he either did not hear, or deliberately chose to ignore. Smith went forward to confront Francis, who picked up a capstan bar to defend himself, in a struggle which followed between the two men, Smith wrestled the bar away from Francis and immediately struck him a hard blow to the head with the make-shift weapon.

Following the blow Francis fell to the deck seriously injured and was taken to his cabin where he died three days later. Smith departed to his cabin where he remained for the rest of the voyage. When the *Cutty Sark* anchored off Anjer Point, on the western tip of Java, Captain Wallace conspired to help his first mate make an escape as the crew were determined to see Smith handed over to the authorities. The captain of an American clipper anchored close by, the *Colorada*, agreed to secretly take Smith aboard as a member of the crew and he was smuggled off the *Cutty Sark* by boat. When the crew of the *Cutty Sark* realised Smith had made his escape they turned on Captain Wallace in open mutiny. Realising the perilous situation he was in and no doubt suffering from the tropical heat and pains of guilt, Captain Wallace jumped off the stern of the ship into the shark infested waters of the Java Sea and he was never seen again. On hearing of the loss of the *Cutty Sark*'s master, John Willis sent a cable out to Captain Fowler on the *Hallowe'en*, anchored at Hong Kong, suggesting that the clipper's first mate be appointed master of the *Cutty Sark*, which Captain Fowler readily agreed to.

The first mate of the *Hallowe'en*, William Bruce, was a competent navigator however he proved to be a poor clipper captain, being much too fond of the drink. His drinking exploits were witnessed by the crew of the *Cutty Sark* after he entered into a drinking bout with the clipper's first mate. Both the men were unpopular with crew of the *Cutty Sark*, who were all worked much harder than was necessary. One unfortunate young apprentice, suffering under the hands of the first mate, was ordered aloft for no good reason, throughout all of his night watches.

The *Cutty Sark*, while commanded by Captain Bruce, seemed to be sailing under a curse, travelling from port to port in pursuit of worthwhile shipment of cargo but never making a decent passage, or bringing home the income John Willis had expected. After failing to secure any worthwhile cargo at Shanghai, cholera broke out aboard ship, and after picking up a cargo of jute from the Philippines bound for America, the *Cutty Sark* ran out of provisions and the crew resorted to begging for rations from any passing vessels they encountered. Luck finally ran out for Captain Bruce when he was relieved of his duties on arrival in New York in April 1882.

Towards the final months of the tea season in 1880, the

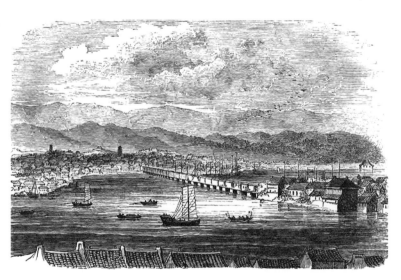

The river port of Foochow, on mainland China became an important trading port during the late 1800s where hundreds of thousands of tons of tea were shipped out to Europe and America.

Hallowe'en and its sister ship *Blackadder* were both at anchor in the port of Foochow loading tea for the run home. The port of Foochow, on the south-east coast of China had come under British occupation at the end of the opium wars and was one of five Chinese treaty ports open to all traders from Europe and America.

After the violent confrontations which had taken place between the British and the Chinese during the war over the opium trade, both nations were now carrying out trading transactions on much more sociable terms, both taking advantage of the rewards the tea trade would bring. The port of Shanghai was much closer to the major tea producing area of Canton, where cargoes of tea could be loaded aboard ships much earlier in the season than clippers taking on cargo from ports further north. The *Blackadder* was the first of the two clippers to make way leaving Foochow on 26 September 1880, followed closely by the *Hallowe'en* sailing six days later on 1 October 1880. The clippers raced each other south towards the South China Sea and out into the Indian Ocean, with the *Hallowe'en*

The Blackadder, *moored off shore during the early 1900s, was considered an unlucky ship to sail upon, where the clipper seemed to encounter mishaps wherever it sailed.*

gradually closing in on its sister ship, pushing the *Blackadder* all the way. Both clippers arrived off the Downs in February 1881, the *Blackadder* just a day ahead of its sister ship, however the *Hallowe'en* had made the quicker passage taking 126 days against the *Blackadder's* 130.

Although making a good run home the *Hallowe'en's* sister ship, *Blackadder*, appeared to be finding mishap wherever it sailed. Whether colliding with other ships, losing masts and rigging or running aground, the clipper gained an unwelcome reputation for demanding life on every voyage. Meanwhile the *Hallowe'en* continued to bring John Willis good fortune and excellent profits. Under the command of Captain Fowler and then under Captain R. F. Douton, who had served his apprenticeship aboard the clipper passing up to second mate, then first mate and master. The *Hallowe'en* continually picked up charters of tea, where the swiftness of the clipper under sail ensured the ship made good runs home even in the severest of weather conditions. The clipper regularly carried home 1,500 tons of tea each voyage, which earned a premium of up to six-pence for every pound in weight aboard ship, securing well earned bonuses for the captain and crew. John Willis had good reason to favour the *Hallowe'en* above all other ships in the company's fleet which he regarded to be his luckiest and most profitable clipper of all.

On 13 August 1886, the *Hallowe'en* was ready to make way from Foochow under the command of Captain Douton, with the ship's complement for the voyage consisting of a first and second mate, a ship's carpenter and a sailmaker, seven able seamen and eight young apprentices all under the age of seventeen. From the outset, bad weather delayed the clipper's departure as strong gales kept the ship trapped on the Min River for five days. Once free from the strong winds there was nothing more than a light breeze to take the *Hallowe'en* out into the East China Sea, where the clipper's progress was hampered by calms and light air. After taking forty-seven days to beat clear of the South China Sea and into the Indian Ocean, the clipper encountered only constant headwinds throughout the remainder of the voyage home, where the crew worked tirelessly to keep the ship moving at the best possible speed, which was exhaustingly hard work for all aboard.

After five months' hard sailing, the *Hallowe'en* was running up into the English Channel when the first mate, James Jackson, sighted the Eddystone lighthouse at 5.30 p.m. on Monday 17 January 1887, at a distance of around twelve miles. The daylight by this time was fading fast and weather conditions were becoming exceedingly poor, with a misty rain reducing visibility. Captain Douton, standing on the poop deck, had not slept for some forty-eight hours, required to remain on duty because of the difficult sailing conditions the ship had encountered making a course northwards towards the Channel. However, once the clipper had sighted the lighthouse, Captain Douton had expected an easy and speedy passage along the Channel to the Downs, the crew looking forward to taking a well earned rest once safely at anchor. There was a south-south-east, force-nine gale blowing as the *Hallowe'en* passed the Eddystone Light making around twelve knots. At 7.35pm, Captain Douton sent the second mate forward to relieve the first mate and to keep lookout for Start Point Lighthouse off the port bow. Once sighting the light the second mate called out that Start Point had been spotted indicating that the clipper was on course, sailing around eight miles off the light. With the wind blowing hard, the *Hallowe'en* was making good headway as the thick swirling mist which had engulfed the clipper began to lift slightly. Almost immediately land was sighted extremely close to the port side, which where cliffs to the west of Sewer Mill Cove on the south Devon coast. Through the grey mist sudden flashes of white appeared at sea level off the clipper's port bow. The crew realised that the flashes seen were in fact the crests of waves breaking across the bay and that the clipper was running perilously close into shore. The Captain immediately gave the order 'All hands on deck' and the crew tried in desperation to adjust sail while the helmsman turned the wheel hard to starboard in an attempt to steer the clipper away from danger, but it was far too late.

At 7.45 p.m., the *Hallowe'en* ran aground close to Sewer Mill Cove and became stuck fast in the sand. The clipper began to roll heavily in the pounding seas which caused a block from the spanker to break free, striking the helmsman at the wheel a heavy blow to his head, severely injuring him. Captain Douton, realising that the ship was stuck fast, ordered one of the ship's boats to be launched in an attempt to get his crew away. However the waves which came crashing in on the stricken vessel made this task impossible. The captain located the position of the nearest coastguard station on the ship's charts, which was a mile distant along the coast and he gave the order to fire the rockets and flares to be lit on deck. To the dismay of the crew, the distress signals were not acknowledged by the coastguard station and in desperation the crew resorted to retrieving clothes and bedding from the cabins which they soaked in lamp oil and set alight on the poop deck, in the hope of signalling any patrolling coastguard on watch. As huge yellow flames shot up into the night sky, large waves continued to break over the ship's forecastle, washing along the deck. The captain, in the fear that his crew may be washed overboard, ordered the men to climb up into the rigging and just as he did so a huge sea suddenly came onto the ship washing away all the boats, parts of forecastle and large sections of the cabin housing, leaving the crew desperately clinging to the rigging of the clipper's mizzen mast.

As the heavy seas continued to pound the *Hallowe'en*, the

Hallowe'en running aground at Sewer Mill Cove, on 17 January 1887.

mizenmast began to groan and creak under the strain and weight of men clinging to the rigging. Fearing that the mast was about to part from the ship, the crew to a man, managed to scramble across to the mainmast. When the mainmast seemed to be about to collapse, the men then all shifted position onto the foremast where they remained for the rest of that traumatic night. Captain Douton had the foresight to grab four bottles of spirits from the cabin before climbing into the rigging, the contents of which, he shared out between his crew, the only comfort they had throughout that night, a night which the crew all assumed would be their last.

That next morning, the crew, wet, cold and completely exhausted, could not believe that none of the ship's party had been lost in the constant deluge of water that had been crashing in over the clipper throughout that night. As the mist began to lift and the morning light broke, the crew could see that the ship had grounded on a bank of sand close to the entrance of the cove, with rocks each side and high cliffs beyond, which in the circumstances, was extremely lucky, as if the ship had grounded either side of the cove and into the rocks, there was no doubt the ship would have broken up and it would have been the end of them all. Nevertheless, the clipper was laying some 100 yards off shore, and the men were still in a perilous situation. Two brave crew members, Second Mate Percival Mclean and Able Seaman Gustav Lichfield, a German seaman who had joined the *Hallowe'en* for the return voyage, volunteered to swim ashore with a line to make up a rig using the ship's yards washed up in the cove to haul each member of the crew ashore.

Mclean, the better swimmer, managed to make it safely to the shore only to lose hold of the line. Lichfield, following after his crewmate, was suddenly dashed against a rocky outcrop by the waves before reaching shore and the crew on the clipper could do no more than watch his lifeless body, face down in the water, wash passed the ship and out to sea.

Another member of ship's crew decided to take to the water and swim ashore with the line and although he managed to reach his crewmate, he had also lost hold of the line in the freezing water. Three more of the ship's crew volunteered to take a line ashore, however fearing for the life of his men Captain Douton refused to give them permission. Thankfully, a local farmer who had been leaving his farm house around half a mile distant, had seen the stricken vessel and made his way to the beach, just as the first crewmen had come ashore. It was now 7.30 a.m. and a local coastguard from the Bolt Head Coastguard Station finally spotted

THIS
LIFEBOAT ESTABLISHMENT
WAS PRESENTED TO THE
ROYAL NATIONAL LIFEBOAT
INSTITUTION
AND ENDOWED IN PERPETUITY
BY THE UNITED GRAND LODGE
OF
FREEMASONS OF ENGLAND
IN COMMEMORATION OF
THE SAFE RETURN FROM INDIA
OF THE MOST WORSHIPFUL
GRAND MASTER
H.R.H. ALBERT EDWARD
PRINCE OF WALES.
1877.

CHARLES H. COOFE.
HON" ARCHITECT

the clipper for the first time.

With the coastguard now fully aware of the ship's plight, the two crewmen, wet, cold, shivering and standing in nothing but their wet shirts, were taken to the local farm to recover, while the coastguard officer ran with all haste to the lifeboat station at Hope Cove to the west of Sewer Mill Cove, where the ship lay wrecked. On the arrival of the Coastguard officer at Hope Cove, the alarm was raised and the Lifeboat *Alexandra* was launched at 8.30 a.m., to attempt to rescue the crew of *Hallowe'en*. The lifeboat made its way with all speed three miles around the coast towards the cove where the clipper had grounded. As the *Alexandra* came within a quarter-mile from the *Hallowe'en* the crew of the clipper, who had spotted the lifeboat first, let out a great cheer. Closing up on the clipper, the lifeboat's coxswain and crew were astonished to see the crew still clinging high up on the rigging of the clipper's foremast. As the lifeboat reached the *Hallowe'en* the coastguard arrived on the beach equipped with a rocket line, which was fired aboard the clipper. In spite of this the crew decided to take their chances of rescue by the lifeboat. Even though the *Alexandra* broke its rudder during the rescue, all the men were taken off the stricken clipper by 11.00 a.m. The last to leave the *Hallowe'en* was the ship's master, Captain Douton.

With no safe place to land the crew on the beach or close to Sewer Mill Cove, the crew of the *Hallowe'en* were taken back in the *Alexandra*, to Hope Cove. On their arrival, the exhausted crew of the clipper were taken into the homes of the villagers, where all were extremely well cared for by their hosts. The survivors from the clipper were the first crew the *Alexandra* had

Hope Cove RNLI station from where the lifeboat Alexandria *was launched on the morning after the* Hallowe'en *ran aground, which rescued all but one of the clippers' crew. The plaque on the lifeboat station wall commemorates it's opening in 1877, ten years before the* Hallowe'en *was wrecked.*

rescued since located at the lifeboat station in 1878, which gave the people of the village a great feeling of pride. The crew of the *Hallowe'en* were all graciously thankful for the care, kindness and consideration shown to them by the people of Hope Cove. Once recovered from their ordeals, the crew were taken to Salcombe, a

The Hallowe'en *lies on its port side off Sewer Mill Cove between the Ham Stone and the shoreline cliffs.*

small shipbuilding town on the Kingsbridge Estuary where they were all found lodgings in the local hostelry by the agents of the Shipwrecked Mariners Society.

Captain Douton received a telegram from John Willis giving the him full power to do what he thought best for all concerned and he immediately handed over the charge of the ship and cargo to the agents of Lloyds, who had recently arrived on the scene from Plymouth. Most of the *Hallowe'en*'s crew were paid off before returning to London by train. On the day of their departure the people of Salcombe came out in their hundreds to cheer and wave the crew off as they left on a steamer which took them to the railway station up river at Kingsbridge.

Three days after the wrecking of the *Hallowe'en,* the body of the German, Gustav Lichfield, was found in the water and brought ashore. The following day an inquest took place at Lower Sewer Farm, close to the cove where the clipper was wrecked. The first mate of the *Hallowe'en,* John Jackson, blamed the death of his shipmate on the failure of the coastguard to spot the distress signals of the *Halloween.* The coastguard defended their lack of action, stating that the guard on duty that night was out on patrol further along the coast where, due to the fog and poor visibility, the signals from

WRECK OF A CLIPPER SHIP AT SEWER MILL.

The full-rigged ship "Halloween," of London, owned by Messrs John Willis and Son, 115, Leadenhall street, and commanded by Capt. R. F. Donton, went ashore at Sewer Mill Cove, near Salcombe, during a thick fog on Monday evening, and is likely to become a total wreck. The "Halloween" is an iron ship, built at Greenhithe in 1870, is of 920 tons register, and of a class formerly known as "China clippers." She sailed from Foochoou, August 13th, but was detained in the river until the 19th by strong gales. After she sailed she met with nothing but light winds and calms in the China Sea, and took forty-seven days beating clear of this part of the Pacific, since which time she had had constant head winds. As soon as she struck she began to roll heavily, and a block from the spanker got free and hit the man at the wheel a heavy blow on the head, causing him severe injury.

Finding his vessel on shore the captain did all he could to attract attention. Consulting his chart he concluded that there was a coastguard station near. He accordingly at once fired off rockets and burnt flare-ups, but was surprised and alarmed to find that no notice was taken of them by any person on shore. Things were looking very alarming on board; a terrible sea was on, and it was making clean breaches over the vessel. Finding that flare-ups and rockets did no good, the crew brought out their clothes and bedding, saturated them with kerosene oil, and set fire to them on the poop deck, a lurid glare shooting up into the night. But though the Bolt Head Coastguard station was only a mile distant, all these efforts to notify their perilous position were unseen by any person on shore, and after everything had been burned out and all possible efforts made without avail, the crew gave it up as hopeless and resigned themselves to their fate, believing it would not be long before all would be drowned. The captain says none of them expected to see the morning. The crew then huddled together in the mizen rigging, shivering with the cold, and expecting every sea that struck the vessel to dash her to pieces. Thinking that they saw signs of the mizen mast giving way, with great difficulty they changed their position

SOME BR

A meeting
Union was h
Newton Abb
to hear and
Stubbs, vica
Principles of
Oxenham (Lt
present were t
St. Aubyn (St
E. W. Langdon
P. Jackson (
Admiral Dawk
(Plymouth), M
Mr. W. Vicary
(Kingsbridge),
Jackson (Camb
Miss E. Skinn
Rev C. W. S
stating that r
reform, was th
which for man
Council. Dr
were offered
bringing the (
with the alter
that the Un
that diocesa
efforts at ref
one result of
secularise on
hallowed by
nation, or to
ments to a bo
be to prefer th
interests of th
fore, the Chu
once more in f
the nation; t
endowments
sacred to relig
in the election
funds, and in
and the best
widened as to
and life of the
ple of Humphre
think that the
position with

Extract from one of many news articles recording the wreck of the tea clipper Hallowe'en which made headlines in local and national newspapers of the time.

the *Hallowe'en* were not seen. The jury found the crewman's death accidental, however concerns raised regarding the effectiveness of only one solitary coastguard officer patrolling four-and-a-half miles of such a dangerous piece of coastline and the Coroner referred these concerns to the coastguard authority. Events of that fateful night made the local news headlines and accounts of the wrecking, rescue and inquest were printed in the local and London shipping news sheets of the day. After the inquest, the body of Gustav Lichfield was buried in the churchyard at Marlborough, a few miles inland from where the *Hallowe'en* lay wrecked.

After the *Hallowe'en* had run ashore, the clipper's back had been broken during the first night of wrecking, the main-mast had come down and all the hatches had been washed away. Laying broadsides towards shore, the clipper's hull remained virtually intact, however the hold, which was packed with 1,600 tons of tea in wooden chests had been submerged below the water. Arrangements were made by the agents for the salvage of the cargo, which Captain Douton valued at £35,000, with the duty on the tea estimated to be around £56,000. The *Hallowe'en* had been valued at £10,000, however true to his word John Willis had not insured the clipper, but he had insured the cargo for £40,000. On the day salvage work began a storm blew up which sent large waves crashing into the bay and over the wreck, breaking up the clipper's hull and the wooden crates spilling the tea out into the water. The loose tea was gradually washed up ashore forming a great wall several feet high across the entrance of Sewer Mill Cove.

The tea was packed into sacks by local farmers who were promised payment by a London agent for carrying out the work and the sacks of tea were loaded onto a steamer for transportation to London. The farmers however went unpaid and the sacks of tea, which would have been in extremely poor condition tainted by salt water, were never seen again. John Willis had lost the clipper he had favoured the most, while the *Blackadder*, never equal to its sister the *Hallowe'en*, sailed on for another eighteen years, until wrecked off the coast of Brazil in November 1905. The only remaining vessel from John Willis & Son's merchant fleet, the *Cutty Sark*, is now in permanent dry dock close to Greenwich Pier, around two miles east along the Thames foreshore, from where the *Hallowe'en* was first launched from Greenwich Marsh.

Sailing into a time of discovery - the Royal Naval ship *Dolphin*

The frigate Dolphin *on patrol in the West Indies – 1762.*

King Henry VIII chose the riverside town of Woolwich, located four miles east of Greenwich Palace, as the site for the building of his first Royal Dockyard in 1512, preceding the Deptford yards by just a year. Henry VIII's intention was to develop the old trading port into a shipyard where he would build the greatest warship ever known, the *Henry Grace à Dieu*. The shipping history of Woolwich pre-dates the building of the Royal Dockyard, where archaeological remains found, suggest the settlement had originated as a small riverside port. The foundations of a Roman fort were discovered close to the dockyard site and the remains of a much earlier Iron Age settlement were also found close by. The Anglo-Saxons were the first to make Woolwich a permanent port community, transporting wool from Kent sheep to the continent by boat. The name of Woolwich is believed to be Anglo-Saxon, meaning 'a trading place of wool'. The riverside port gradually developed into a large military establishment through shipbuilding and armaments manufacturing. Henry VIII commissioned his Royal Dockyards to be built adjacent to the Royal Arsenal, established in 1471 for the manufacture of arms to supply England's fighting forces.

The first ship commissioned at the yard, *Henry Grace à Dieu* better known as the *Great Harry*, was built by Henry VIII in honour of his father, Henry VII. The ship, built to the designs of an English carrack, was a contemporary of the *Mary Rose*, however the *Great*

Woolwich Royal Dockyard with several warships on the slips and in dock, c.1788.

Harry was even larger weighing almost 1,500 tons and measuring 165 feet in length, the biggest English warship ever built up to that time. The *Great Harry* was constructed by foreign shipwrights who arrived in England after the King had invited the best shipbuilders from all of Europe to come to England and build this impressive warship. A majority of these shipwrights and craftsmen came from Italy where the progress in the design and construction of ships, had surpassed those of their English counterparts.

Drawing of the Great Harry, Henri Grace De Dieu, *presented to Henry VIII in 1547, a year before the King died.*

When Henry VIII's daughter Elizabeth came to the throne, she continued on her father's shipbuilding quest, improving and maintaining the dockyard facilities and the adjacent Royal Arsenal, where both military sites would gradually transform the whole of the area of Woolwich into a prosperous shipbuilding and military town. The continued development of the yards included the building of slipways, dry docks, workshops, a foundry, a metal working factory, a gun bastion and storehouses. As the dockyards and armaments site expanded, new properties were built in the town to accommodate the increasing population moving into the area to take up a range of work opportunities.

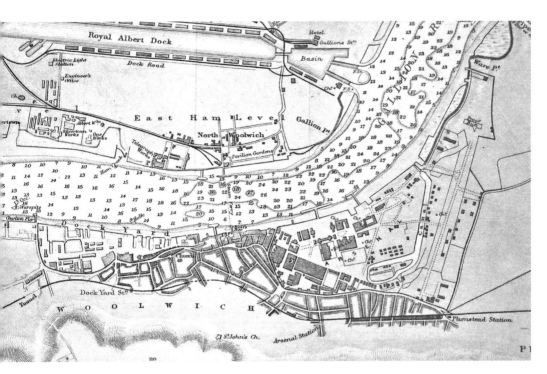

The Woolwich Royal Dockyards became the birthplace of many great hearts of oak made famous by their adventures on the oceans and seas all around the world. The *Vanguard*, the *Elizabeth* and the *Ark Royal* were three of these ships built at Woolwich which were in action against the Spanish Armada. The name of *Ark Royal*, flagship of the fleet commanded by Charles Howard, would be proudly carried by a succession of British-built warships in remembrance of the part this great ship played in the defeating Spain's attempted invasion of England.

The victory over the Spanish Armada was the result of superior seamanship of the English crews, the speed and manoeuvrability of the smaller English vessels and assistance from the winds and tides. Following the defeat of Spain, warships designed and built by English master-craftsmen became much larger and more powerfully armed in an attempt to enforce English domination of the seas.

The Pett family dynasty of Master Shipwrights had been designing and building ships at both Deptford and Woolwich Royal Dockyards since the reign of Elizabeth I. Joseph Pett was the Master Shipwright when Sir Francis Drake's ship, the *Defiance*, put into Woolwich Dockyard to have its hull sheathed, before sailing on his last voyage to the West Indies. Joseph's younger brother Phineas was one of the carpenters employed at the dockyard which worked on Drake's ship; this young carpenter

Woolwich dockyard prior to closure in 1869. To the right is the Royal Woolwich Arsenal which continued to produce armaments until the mid-1900s.

became one of the most renowned Master Shipwrights of his time and was later appointed Master of the Corporation of Shipwrights, designing and building ships for Sir Walter Raleigh, James I and Charles I, at Woolwich Royal Dockyards.

The Pett shipwrights resided at various properties in Kent and South London, moving as required to oversee their shipbuilding

Galley moored at a Mediterranean port – 1676. (Abraham Stock)

projects in the dockyards on the Thames and Medway. The shipwrights leased a large area of woodland in north Kent, 'Petts Wood', around ten miles south of Woolwich, for felling of oak trees required for the construction of English men-of-war.

In 1610, the *Prince Royal*, a fifty-five gun ship designed and built by Phineas Pett, was launched from the Woolwich dockyard slipway, the first British warship built with three gundecks, a revolutionary design at the time. Previous naval warships had been designed along the lines of Venetian galleys, well suited for the calmer waters of the Mediterranean and coastal cruising, but were not well suited for the rigours of long voyages or sailing in northern waters. The ships were extremely top heavy with high forecastles and poop

decks and Phineas Pett's new ship designs disposed of these high structures where these radical new designs influenced the way all wooden warships would be built in the future.

A second three-decker, the *Sovereign of the Seas*, designed and built by Phineas Pett and his son Peter at Woolwich, was commissioned by Charles I at a cost £65,586. The vessel became the finest and most extravagantly decorated English warship ever built, however the funds spent on its construction created a financial crisis for the King, which contributed to the onset of the Civil War. When war broke out, Peter Pett decided to back the Parliamentarians rather than his King, after he had already received payment for building the ship.

Peter Pett succeeded Phineas to become a Master-Shipwright, relying on his father's guidance to carry on the family traditions of designing and building warships at Woolwich Royal Dockyards. He took his father's shipbuilding innovations to a new level when he designed and built the *Constant Warwick*, launched in 1645. The ship, a thirty-two-gun privateer, was regarded to have been the first English-built fighting frigate.

At the time of the Battle of Trafalgar, Britain's fighting ships were considered the finest to have sailed the oceans of the world under

A three-decker Spanish warship, at anchor off Naples in 1669. The Spanish ships were considered far superior to British-built vessels of the time. (Abraham Willaerts)

the flag of the Royal Navy, however this was not always the case. By the early 1700s, ship design and construction had not moved forward since ships designed by the Pett shipwright dynasty. As ships increased in size and power they did not necessarily increase in seaworthiness. By the early eighteenth century, British-built fighting ships had become inferior to the French and Spanish vessels encountered by the Royal Navy in minor skirmishes and parochial wars around the globe. The Admiralty had been relying on the superior sailing expertise of its ships' officers and able seamen, rather than on the quality of its ships to win these encounters at sea. Both French and Spanish ships were prizes worthy of capture and when manned by Royal Naval crews they became an even more effective fighting vessel than when sailed under the flag of their own nation. British ships rolled and pitched about mercilessly in heavy seas while captured prize ships, sailed with ease, even in the roughest of weather, which meant their guns were more effective when fired from a stable platform.

The Admiralty appointed a committee of flag officers and Commissioners to instruct the dockyard's Master Shipwrights to design a new rated system for fighting ships, to formulated and specified sets of plans. The Admiralty formed a board of Establishment in 1706 to standardise the design and size of naval ships and a six-step rating system was put into place. Before this, shipwrights would build ships through knowledge handed down through generations of shipbuilders, their own ingenuity and a

The Royal James *was built at Woolwich in 1658 by master shipwright Christopher Pett. Originally named the* Richard, *after Richard Cromwell to honour his appointment of Protector after succeeding his late father Oliver Cromwell, the ship was refitted out as a first-rate ship after the restoration in 1660 and renamed and re-registered for the new English Royal Navy.*

general rule of thumb, where naval vessels were built in varied sizes and carried a varying amount of guns. Under the new rating system, ships of the line referred to naval vessels rated according to fighting capability with no less than sixty-four mounted heavy guns. First-raters carried 100-guns or more, from twelve-pounders up to heavy thirty-two-pounders, second-raters carried around ninety-guns and third-raters, a minimum of sixty-four-guns. Fourth-raters down to sixth-raters carried up to sixty guns and these ships were used in a variety of roles, from escort duties to commerce raiders. Naval engagements were fought out between the largest ships of the line and as most seas battles would be won by the Navy with larger and more heavily armed vessels, the natural progression was to build bigger and more powerfully armed warships.

The committee's results continued to be poor and new ships built showed hardly any improvement from previous vessels. When Vice Admiral George Anson was appointed First Lord of the Admiralty, he wasted no time in not only improving the Royal Dockyard's administration, but more importantly, he made extensive improvements in shipbuilding at the yards. The Vice Admiral had seen how the captured prizes had outperformed their ships and insisted that these prizes were used as models in the design of Admiralty-built fighting ships. Steadily the Admiralty ships improved in design, sailing quality and fighting capability. During a period of time when Britain was relatively free from conflict and wars with other nations, large heavily armed ships of the line were rarely needed, however to maintain British naval control of the sea, the Admiralty required a force of economically-built ships to fly the nation's flag in the furthest parts of the world. The Admiralty was quick to acknowledge the usefulness of the naval frigates with their origins dating back to the *Constant Warwick*, designed and built by Peter Pett. Fast and highly manoeuvrable, quick and economical to build, frigates were able to sail independently from the fleet and were useful in times of peace and times of war. Throughout the eighteenth century and early part of the nineteenth century, the Royal Dockyards were employed in the construction of hundreds of these highly prized small fighting vessels, considered the hardest working ships of the Royal Navy. A posting to a frigate was a much sought-after position, as these vessels were involved in plenty of action, bringing a fair share of prize money and promotion for officers and crew.

Under the new Admiralty Establishment of 1745, succeeding the Admiralty Establishments of 1706, a new sixth-rated frigate

The Royal Naval red ensign flown by the navy's most senior squadron during the seventeenth century and the eighteenth century. The navy adopted three colours of ensign; red, blue and white for each of its three squadrons. At the Battle of Trafalgar, Nelson's squadron had flown the white ensign and in 1846 the navy abandoned the three flag system, preferring to use the white ensign on all Royal Naval ships.

was commissioned to be built at the yards of Earlsman Sparrow, a private contractor at Rotherhithe. When the naval dockyards were full to capacity, private shipyards took on commissions for the building of Royal Navy ships. Earlsman Sparrow accepted the Admiralty contract in October 1747 while completing the final stages of the *Queenborough*, a frigate which was launched in January 1748. When Earlsman Sparrow began building the frames for the yard's latest commission, the shipbuilders were already in financial difficulties through building the *Queenborough*, which resulted in the shipbuilders facing bankruptcy. When the yards were forced to

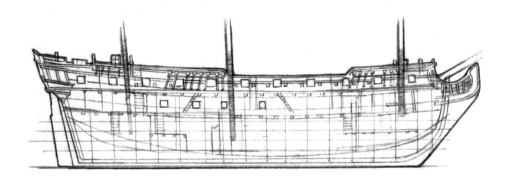

close, the order was then transferred to Woolwich Royal Dockyard in June 1748 and the frigate's frames were transported to Woolwich with the commission taken on by the yard's Master Shipwright Thomas Fellowes.

1745 Establishment plans 'Approved by the Flag Officers' of the sixth-rate, twenty-four gun frigate Dolphin.

Thomas Fellowes had been appointed the yard's Master Shipwright two years before and had overseen the building and launch of the *Bristol*, a fifty-gun fourth-rate ship. The new frigate's frames were re-erected at the yard and the keel was laid down on 3 August 1748. The shipwrights, carpenters, joiners and craftsmen working on the frigate at the yard were highly experienced in building these types of fighting vessels, working to the precise details laid out in Admiralty plans and design specifications under the directions of the yard's Master Shipwright. The frigate's keel measured eighty-eight feet in length, with the overall length of the vessel measuring 113 feet. The beam – the width of the vessel – measured thirty-two feet and the ship's hold was eleven feet in depth. The frigate's carrying capacity was rated at just over 500 tons, designed to carry twenty-four-guns, twenty nine-pounders on

Royal Naval ship off Woolwich dockyard during the mid-1700s, with several warships under construction on the slips and in the dry docks. To the right can be seen the tall vertical poles erected to assist hoisting up the ship's heavy timbers.

the upperdeck, two nine-pounders on the aft lowerdeck and two three-pounders on the quarterdeck. The frigate's gun deck was now used for crew accommodation, with the main armament positioned on the upper deck, or weather deck.

The frigate's gun power and role these vessels played during active duty had determined the way the vessel was designed and built. The main guns of a sixth-rate frigate were positioned on its upper decks above the waterline, making the vessel an effective gun platform, however this resulted in the vessel becoming top heavy. To balance out the ship's weight, ballast was loaded deep down in the hull of the ship. When engaged in an action, the frigate needed to retain stability so its guns could still be brought to bear, without losing mobility when sailing close to the wind. These conflicting design objectives would determined the frigate's length, breadth,

draft, hull shape, sail and rigging layout.

The timber from over 200 oak trees felled for the building of a frigate and the selection of the trees used, was the responsibility of the dockyard's Master Shipwright. Thomas Fellowes took regular trips to Shooters Hill, south of Woolwich Dockyards, to choose the best oaks growing in Oxleas Wood, an area of ancient forest dating back some 8,000 years. Once cut, the timber from these great oaks were transported down from Shooters Hill to the dockyards where the cut timbers were soaked in long deep ponds to ensure the planks were well seasoned and would not split or shrink once fitted. After the keel was laid the shipwrights and carpenters began building the ship's stern post and stem posts. Both merchant ships and war ships from the same period were constructed using similar tried and trusted methods and traditional shipbuilding skills. As the

hull began taking shape, the soaked planks were put over fires and bent into the required shape before nailed into position. While the frigate's hull was under construction the rudder, gratings, hatches, capstan and masts were being built in the dockyard workshops.

Timber used for the ship's masts were put through the same soaking process as the rest of the ship's timbers, submerged in the dockyard's mast ponds. At one time ships' masts came from the trunk of a single fir tree, a pole mast, then by the sixteenth century as ships increased in size, much higher and stouter mast were needed. Each mast was now made up in three sections, the

Above: *Dockyard carpenter making ready the ship's timbers.*

Right: *Building and hooping the ship's masts in the dockyard workshops. The shipbuilding industry in the Royal dockyard offered plenty of opportunities for shipwrights, carpenters, caulkers, joiners, sailmakers, riggers and general labourers to earn a steady, if meagre, income from building naval warships, where over 100 men were employed in each ship's construction.*

lower mast, topmast and top-gallant mast. Because of the increase in the height of the masts, the lower mast required a much larger circumference than a single polemast could provide, which resulted in the lower mast being made up in separate lengths of timber, dovetailed together and securely bound by iron hoops and close turns of rope. Fighting ships' masts were much taller than the masts of a merchant vessel of the same tonnage; a characteristic which set naval vessels apart from a merchantman.

The other noticeable difference between both types of vessels was the decorations which adorned their beakheads and galleries. Merchant ships had elaborate and expensively carved designs, compared to the relatively plain decorations of a naval ship, although both types of vessel carried superbly carved figureheads on the ship's beakhead, or prow. During the sixteenth century, fighting ships had carried the traditional lion figurehead gilded or painted bright red. In 1703, the Admiralty made an order that all ships below first-rate would carry this style figurehead rather than a figurehead which depicted the name of the ship.

On 6 December 1748, six months after the frigate's keel was laid down, the Admiralty issued the frigate with the name *Dolphin*; the ninth British naval vessel to bear the title. In the best naval traditions, the names issued to new commissioned ships were taken

from a previous Royal Navy vessel, which had served the nation with honour and distinction, either lost in action, or decommissioned. The names of ships lost through negligence, collision, grounding, sinking or wrecking would never be used by any other Royal Naval vessel again.

The shipwrights and carpenters, who worked on the frigate, took their orders from Thomas Fellowes, who in turn needed to take instruction from the Admiralty throughout the whole shipbuilding process, ensuring the ship was built exactly to Admiralty Establishment standards. On one occasion the Master Shipwright needed to request directions from the Admiralty on the installation of the ship's fireplace and whether it was to be fitted in the same manner as the fireplace on the *Deptford*, a frigate built at the Royal Dockyard at Deptford. The Master Shipwright then needed to request directions from the Admiralty to make an order for the Master Smith at Deptford to make a similar fireplace for the *Dolphin*. All of these orders and requests from

Left: Ship's capstan built in the yard's workshop and consisted of a wooden drum mounted on an iron axle, used mainly to haul ropes and raise anchors.

Right: Carved and gilded decorations expertly created by the dockyard's skilled craftsmen.

the Master Shipwright required the approval of the Admiralty Ordinance Board as the finances required to pay for the work carried out at the yards and in purchasing equipment and supplies were under the Admiralty's strict control. Before Admiral Anson began to implement the much-needed reforms in shipbuilding and dockyard administration, the operations at the dockyards were open to corruption and bribery through private deals carried out between the dockyard officials and suppliers. However, at the time

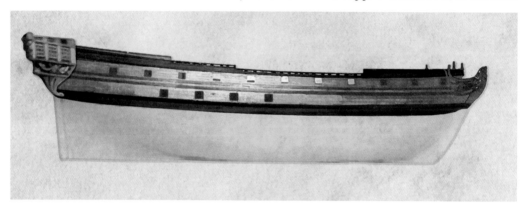

Half-hull of a 130 to 150 foot frigate from the mid-1700s, carrying up to thirty guns, decorated in traditional Royal Naval colours.

the *Dolphin* was under construction, the yards were running to a precision as would be expected of the Royal Navy.

While the *Dolphin* remained on the slip, the yard had three other vessels under construction, where shipwrights, carpenters, painters and labourers moved from one ship to the next, as and when their services were required. It would be essential for fighting ships to be built as quickly as possible in times of war, however during periods of peace, the completed hull of a ship would often be left on the slips, sometimes for up to a year, to allow for shrinkage and settling. On completion of the ship's hull and decks, the seams between the planking would be sealed with oakum – tarred hemp rope – and the hull was then coated in boiling pitch, making the hull watertight and rigid. While on the slips the ship's steering gear was fitted, where the rudder was operated by a large double wheel, drum and rope and pulley system giving the vessel much greater manoeuvrability.

By the summer of 1750, the hull of the *Dolphin* was complete and ready for priming and painting. As with most naval frigates of the time, the *Dolphin* would be painted in traditional naval colours. The hull below the waterline would be painted with a white compound made from tallow, sulphur and resin to help repel the wood-boring ship worms, the gunwale would be painted black and the topsides were creamy yellow along the length of the gun ports, made from a mixture of ochre and white oil paint. The frigate remained on the slips for almost a year, prior to launch, during which time the dockyard came under the supervision of Master Shipwright, Thomas Corbett, who informed the Admiralty in April 1751 that he was proposing to launch the *Dolphin* on the last springtide of the month when the river would be at its deepest and widest. The launching of Woolwich-built Royal Naval ships were extremely popular ceremonial occasions, attracting crowds of spectators arriving in their thousands on the day to witness this launching spectacle.

When Royal Naval ships were launched, it would be customary for a member of the Royal Family, or a Senior Admiralty Official, to sponsor the ship, which involved naming the frigate when breaking a bottle of wine across the bow, as the vessel rolled down the slipway and into the water. The custom replaced an earlier tradition of drinking a toast from a large jewelled silver standing cup which was then tossed overboard, after the remainder of the contents had been emptied out over the ship's forward deck, following the naming of the ship. The tradition died out during the 1600s due to the costs involved in producing these expensive decorative cups, which would be lost overboard at the launch.

The traditional ceremonial standing cup which was used up until the late seventeenth century to bless the ship at launch.

On 1 May 1751, a large crowd of enthusiastic spectators gathered around the dockyard and slipway while others packed onto small riverboats, bobbing about on the river. A group of smartly dressed Admiralty officers and officials stood upon the ship's deck waiting for the signal to release the ship. An hour before high tide, the Master Shipwright gave the awaited order and the launching party began the task of driving out the blocks and wedges from under the *Dolphin*'s keel and cutting away the shores and stanchions retaining the ship. With the shores cut, the frigate gradually slid down the slipway and a great cheer came up from the crowd as the ship smoothly entered the water, ensign, jack and pennant flying proudly from the ship's deck. A bottle of wine was broken across the vessel's bow and the frigate was officially christened the *Dolphin*.

With the successful launch and ceremonies over, the frigate was taken in tow to its moorings, ready for fitting out. The costs of building the frigate up to its launch had come to £8,545.0.6*d*, with the total cost of the ship coming to £11,872.12.8*d*, after fitting out. The fitting out of the frigate took just over a year, including the installation of the ship's masts and rigging. The ship's interior,

Launch of the Thunderer at the Royal Woolwich dockyard in 1831. Even though hundreds of ships were launched from the yards during almost 300 years of shipbuilding, the crowds would regularly attend ship launchings in their thousands.

although built to the highest specifications by the Royal Dockyard craftsmen, were not as extravagantly decorated as those found on a merchantman of the same period. The captain and officers' quarters were located aft in the galleries, with the crew accommodation, galley and small arms store on the lowerdeck. The ship's hold, below the lowerdeck, was fitted out for the storage of provisions, supplies, sails, rope, armaments and ammunition.

After the frigate's completion and successful sea trials, the *Dolphin* was commissioned for service in May 1752, under the command of Captain Richard Howe, with orders to sail for the Straits of Gibraltar. However, at the beginning of June, the ship was still docked at Woolwich awaiting further supplies ordered by the frigate's captain. Reluctantly, Captain Howe had to request permission from the Admiralty for the *Dolphin*'s crew be lodged aboard another ship until the frigate was ready to sail. Captain Howe had made a name for himself in the service of the Royal Navy at only nineteen years of age while in command of a sloop patrolling the North Sea in 1745. Coming across two French privateers, Captain Howe's sloop, accompanied by a Royal Naval frigate, engaged both vessels, where in the action that followed, the young naval officer was severely wounded in the head. After recovering from his injuries, Captain

Howe was appointed commander of his own frigate patrolling the islands of the West Indies taking on pirates and privateers. This daring Naval captain was then appointed the commander of a third-rate ship of the line, where in a battle with Spanish ships off Havana he captured a sixty-four-gun Spanish frigate, bringing him, his officers and crew, a welcome share of prize money. The officers and crew of naval ships were dependent on securing prize money distributed throughout the ship's complement by seniority and rank, to supplement their meagre wages. Royal Naval officers received around £10 a month, dependant on position and rank and a regular able seaman was paid twenty-four shillings a month, quarter the pay of merchant seaman. These wages were often held back and paid in arrears as an inducement to prevent desertions. When Captain Howe was appointed the commander of the *Dolphin*, the frigate's crew were made up from men who had sailed with him on previous voyages, following their captain to whatever ship he had been assigned to – a posting to a frigate also offered more opportunities to earn prize money.

Captain Richard Howe. 1726 – 1799, first commander of the Dolphin *for the ship's maiden voyage. Howe joined the navy at the age of thirteen years and was appointed First Lord of the Admiralty in 1783 after a long and distinguished career.*

The rations on board a naval ship were much the same as supplied to the hands on a merchantman, consisting of a ration of salt pork, salt beef, dried fish, oatmeal and dried biscuits, 'hardtack', made from a mixture of flour and water and which were often baked several months in advance of a ship sailing. The hardtack was infested with weevils, small worms, which were knocked out of the biscuits before eating by banging them hard down on the mess table. Along with rations of water, which often became stale and unpalatable after a few months at sea, the crew of a navy ship from the officers down to the cabin boy were issued with a gallon of beer a day and a measure of rum.

A majority of naval vessel cooks prepared the most basic of meals at sea, which hardly varied from day to day. Servings consisted of salted or dried meats boiled up with whatever fresh or dried vegetables were available at the time. The captain had his own private cook and the ship's officers' meals were prepared by a servant. The officers were also afforded certain privileges which allowed them extra food rations, including joints of lamb and beef freshly butchered from livestock kept aboard ship. When provisions were running short, the hands resorted to catching and eating the ship's rats. A good ship's captain however, would look after the welfare of all his men by providing the best rations available throughout long voyages, which not only kept the crew happy and healthy, but also ensured the ship continued to be well run and maintained. Most disciplinary action carried out during a voyage came about through crew members becoming drunk and disorderly after consuming too much rum, which resulted in the Admiralty making an order to issue the crew grog, a ration of rum diluted with water, in an attempt to keep men sober. On long sea voyages to distant lands the ship's stores were replenished with local tropical fruits, vegetables, meat and fish, some of which the crew would never have encountered before.

On 29 July 1752, the *Dolphin* was ready for sea. The frigate's complement consisted of around 160 men including officers, midshipmen, boswains, cooks, surgeon, carpenter, gunners, able

Left: *Ship's galley. A naval frigate was completely self-contained as the frigate's varied duties often required men and ships spending long periods of time at sea.*

Right: *Captain's great cabin, laid out with the best cut glass, chinaware and silverware, where the ship's commander would entertain the frigate's officers.*

seamen, ordinary seamen, marines and boy sailors. Aboard ship, the senior officers were berthed in quarters located aft of the ship in the stern gallery. The captain's spacious accommodation consisted of a great cabin, where he would entertain his officers and a day room with a sleeping berth. Forward of the captain's quarters were the senior officers' cabins, with the junior officers berthed on the lower deck in order of seniority, separated from the ordinary crew and marines. While the officers were afforded wooden racked bunks with mattresses or swinging cots in their own cabins, the remainder of the crew and marines aboard slept in hammocks on the lower deck, which were taken down after use and lashed in nets to the side of the deck, acting as protection against splinters when engaged in battle. The ordinary and able seamen would mess together in groups of around twelve, at removable tables on the same deck where they slept.

For those in the lower order of society, who had no prospects apart from a life of destitution or crime, serving on a ship of the Royal Navy offered them a better standard of living than they would have found ashore, supplied with three square meals a day and plenty of beer and grog to drink. While serving under a good ship's commander set on promotion, which came from successful actions and prizes won, the ship's hands, whether officer or ordinary seaman, could make themselves a very nice sum of money from captured prizes, although life aboard could also be extremely hard and in many cases cruel and brutal. Crews worked in watches measured by four-hour sandglass timers and were marked each half hour by the ringing of a bell, one bell for the first half-hour, two bells for the second half-hour, this would be repeated throughout each watch. Life on a fighting ship brought many hazards where officers

 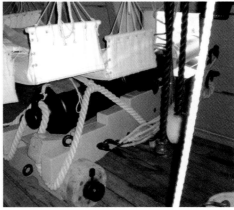

and crew risked severe injury or death while carrying out their duties especially during times of war. Sailors who lost an arm or a leg, who did not die from the injury, were able to carry on in service by having artificial limbs fitted and if they lost an eye then a simple patch was worn and they were required to get on with their duties. Those who suffered long term injuries and were unable to continue in the service had the opportunity to be cared for at palatial Royal Seaman's Hospital in Greenwich, where the living conditions were in stark contrast to the conditions found aboard ship. The residents had their own quarters and earned their keep and pay by carrying out light duties and chores at the hospital, which also included the opportunity to earn extra wages employed in the brewing of beer. The Greenwich Hospital residents would then spend their earnings on tobacco and drink in the local hostelries entertaining regulars with tales of adventures at sea. Experienced long serving able seamen were highly valued by ships' commanders and officers, as crews which served together on previous voyages became a close

Left: Captain's day cabin. The space which ran across the width of the ship's stern gallery would be divided by removable panels for daytime and night time use.

Right: Crew's quarters on the ship's lower deck, or gun deck, where men slept in hammocks or swinging cots suspended above the deck.

hard working unit, reliable and efficient when called upon to do their duty. By the mid-1700s, able seamen had the opportunity to earn promotion and rise up through the ranks to become officers, a system of advancement which had not been previously possible in the Royal Navy.

Captain Howe's orders were to sail with the Mediterranean Fleet, one of the most prestigious and sought after naval postings in the service. Since the early 1600s Barbary and Moorish pirates had been attacking British trade interests in the Mediterranean, capturing merchant ships and ransoming their crews. The Royal Navy patrolled these waters to intercept and capture pirates and privateers intent on attacking British merchant shipping and disrupting trading interests. When the *Dolphin* sailed south in July 1752, towards the warmer climate of the Mediterranean Sea, an uneasy peace was being maintained through treaties agreed between Britain and the Moors. During the next twelve months, the *Dolphin* cruised the waters of the Mediterranean to protect British merchant vessels which came under attack from Moorish pirates not prepared to abide by this treaty. However the frigate saw little action throughout this time while escorting merchant ships from one port to another. Captain Howe then received orders to sail for the Moroccan coastal port of Sallee to meet with representatives of the Moroccan Empire seeking guarantees that the treaty of peace and friendship would continue, which placed the *Dolphin* in an extremely dangerous position, sailing into a potentially hostile port, occupied by Moorish pirates and privateers.

After the death of the King of Morocco in 1727, the empire had become an unstable alliance of tribes struggling for political

A Royal Naval frigate about to capture a privateer, which would bring the captain, officers and crew a large and profitable share of prize money.

and military power where any British ship sailing into their coastal waters was liable to come under hostile attack. The British Government had become increasingly concerned about the internal conflicts taking place within the Moroccan Regime, which could have had serious consequences for Britain's trade and commercial interests in the Mediterranean. On arrival at Sallee, Captain Howe met with representatives of the Moorish Empire where his negotiations ensured the treaty would continue to be honoured, allowing British ships to continue trading without threat of attack. On conclusion of the talks, the *Dolphin* sailed from the port of Sallee, mission successfully accomplished. Over the next few months while the *Dolphin* continued its patrolling duties in the Mediterranean, the parochial conflicts and hostilities which had been taking place between England and France broke out into open war over the colonies in the Americas, which resulted in the outbreak of the Seven Years' War and the *Dolphin* was pressed into action at the outset.

Towards the end of 1755, the British Ministry of War had received intelligence that the French were building up their forces in the Mediterranean with the intention of attacking the British naval base and garrison, Fort St Philip, at Minorca. The British Government had been slow to react to this information and it was not until early March the following year that the Admiralty ordered

British Royal Naval ship at anchor in the Mediterranean, while on patrol protecting British trading interests – 1753. (Claude-Joseph Vernet)

a squadron of ships under the command of Admiral John Byng to sail for Minorca to protect the important naval base and garrison.

The *Dolphin*, now under the command of Captain Carr Scrope, had taken up station at Minorca with a small squadron of ships, commanded by Captain George Edgcumbe. The squadron consisted of two ships of the line, two frigates, including the *Dolphin* and a fighting sloop. Captain Scrope was issued orders from his squadron commander to go ashore in the *Dolphin*'s barge with a party of crewmen and marines to assist with the building of the garrison's defensive works. He commander was then to remain ashore acting as signal officer until Admiral Byng's fleet arrived, with the frigate's first lieutenant, Benjamin Marlow, taking over temporary command of the *Dolphin*.

A force of French soldiers landed at the north of the island on 18 April 1756, joined within two days by the whole of the French army. With no resistance encountered, the French marched on to the British-held naval port and garrison at Mahon to the east of the island.

With a fleet of French warships soon expected, the French began to lay siege to the garrison. Captain Edgcumbe ordered his small squadron to sail for the British base at Gibraltar, capturing several French merchant vessels in the harbour on the way. However, the *Dolphin*'s commander, Captain Scrope and the frigate's shore party were left behind at the garrison, entrenched and under fire.

When Admiral Byng arrived at Gibraltar with his fleet, which included ten ships of the line, Captain Edgcumbe's squadron joined the fleet and the British Naval force sailed for Minorca. On 19 May 1756, Admiral Byng's fleet sighted the garrison and the *Dolphin*,

under the command of Benjamin Marlow, accompanied by the frigates *Phoenix* and *Chesterfield*, were ordered to sail ahead and into the harbour to attempt to make contact with Captain Scrope and the beleaguered British forces at the garrison fort. As the frigates sailed into the harbour, the French fleet was sighted advancing towards the British line of ships. A signal was made for the frigates to return before the British fleet sailed out to meet the oncoming French. The following day, the British and French fleets engaged each other in a fierce exchange of broadsides, where a fire-fight continued throughout the afternoon.

Although the ships in the Admiral Byng's fleet were equal in number to those of the French fleet, they deployed differing fighting tactics. While the British gunners targeted the French ships' guns and hulls, the French preferred to concentrate fire on the British ships' masts and rigging. Eventually the French fleet disengaged, sailing away from the action without sustaining any serious damage, however a majority of ships in Admiral Byng's fleet were left with masts, yards and rigging all shot away. Both French and British fleets had lost many men during the action. However, the French did not lose any high ranking officers, where the British fleet had two of its most experienced captains killed in the engagement.

Admiral Byng remained at station off Minorca for another four days while repairs were carried out to the damaged ships, then without making any further attempt to contact the garrison, which remained under constant bombardment from French mortars and cannons, Admiral Byng ordered the fleet to return to Gibraltar leaving the garrison fort to its fate. The British held out at the garrison until 29 June 1756, when

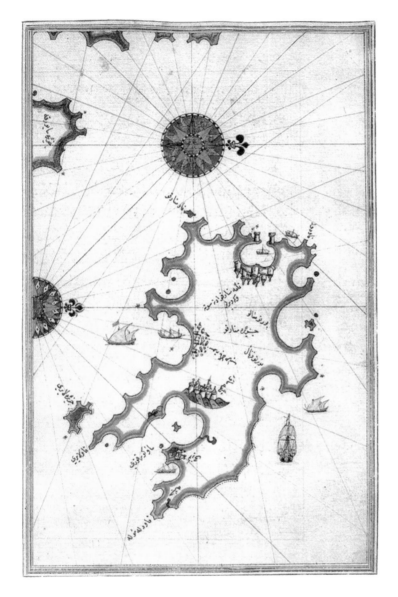

Sixteenth-century chart of Minorca drawn by Turkish cartographer Piri Reis, showing the Port of Mahon and the harbour located on the east coast, towards the bottom of the island as viewed. Inhabited since prehistoric times, Minorca became a powerful base in the Mediterranean and was continuously fought over by opposing nations.

they were forced to initiate terms of surrender after the continued onslaught from the French batteries. The British force within the garrison, which included Captain Scrope and his men from the *Dolphin*, were allowed a safe passage to England after the French took control of Minorca – one of Britain's most important bases in the Mediterranean. The garrison fort, harbour and the whole of the island of Minorca remained under French control until the end of the Seven Years' War.

The Admiralty placed the loss of the garrison and island squarely upon the shoulders of Admiral Byng who was immediately ordered to return to England. On his arrival Admiral Byng was placed in confinement at Greenwich before being transported to Portsmouth to face a court martial. Acquitted of personal cowardice, the Admiral was however condemned to death by firing squad for not carrying out his duty as expected. On 14 March 1757, Admiral Byng was placed in front of a firing squad aboard the *Monarch* in Portsmouth harbour, where at the appointed time a signal was given and a company of Marines opened fire. Five shots struck the Admiral, with one passing straight through his heart killing him instantly, his lifeless body falling down upon the ship's deck. After

'The English Lion dismembered' a cartoon depicting the British public's demand for an enquiry into the loss of Minorca to the French. Admiral Byng is shown towards the left of the cartoon making his plea in front of the Admiralty examiners.

THE ENGLISH LION DISMEMBER'D

Or the Voice of the Public for an enquiry into the loss of Minorca – with Ad: B...g's plea before his Examiners.

Admiral Byng's body was carried away, a bucket of sea water was used to wash his blood from deck. Following the execution there was suspicion and speculation that the Ministry of War had sought to deflect the blame for the loss of Minorca away from the ministry and on to Admiral Byng.

After his return to England, Captain Scrope was posted to another ship, receiving £500 compensation for losses sustained when in command of the *Dolphin* and during the siege of the British garrison at Fort St Philip in the Battle of Minorca. The *Dolphin* remained at its station in Gibraltar under temporary command of Captain Matthew Moore, one of the officers sent out by the Admiralty to replace those ordered home as witnesses for the court martial of Admiral Byng, which included the *Dolphin*'s first lieutenant Benjamin Marlow. On his return to Gibraltar in February 1757, Captain Marlow was appointed commander of the *Dolphin.*

The frigate's role was now to patrol home waters, to protect and defend British merchant shipping coming under attack from French privateers. During these patrols, when any unidentified ship was sighted, the duty of the *Dolphin* would be to close up on the vessel and fire a shot, signalling the unidentified ship to show its colours by raising its nation's flag. If the ship ignored the request or tried to sail away the frigate would give chase, making ready to board the unidentified vessel to inspect its papers. In the likely event that a fire-fight would take place, the captain would give the order to 'clear for action' where everything loose on deck which could splinter into deadly shards of wood if struck by gunfire, was stowed away or towed astern in the ship's boats. Splinter nets were then laid out and the deck was sanded and wet down with seawater, while the ship's guns were made ready for action. The guns were primed with gunpowder and loaded with ammunition, which consisted of either roundshot, barshot, or grapeshot. During engagements, the frigate's marines took up position in the ship's fighting tops, platforms high up on ships' masts, where at close quarters tthey fired down with their muskets on the enemy ship, attempting to hit the officers, gunners, helmsman and snipers.

Under the command of Captain Benjamin Marlow, an ambitious and courageous naval officer, the crew of the *Dolphin* was assured of seeing some action, hoping to secure a fair share of prize money. The first opportunity came in May 1757, while patrolling home waters off Dunkirk, when a lookout on the *Dolphin* spotted a sail on the horizon. Captain Marlow gave orders to intercept the vessel, the twelve-gun Frenchman *La Marquise du Barail*, which the *Dolphin* took as its first prize. The crew of a frigate could make more than their annual pay capturing a prize ship, either merchantman, fighting vessel, pirate or privateer and frigate captains were reluctant to give the order to sink a vessel unless absolutely necessary as a ship was worth more afloat than sunk. A majority of encounters resulted in ships' rigging, masts and spars being shot away, or guns damaged in an attempt to disable the ship. The crew would risk life and limb to board a ship and take it for the prize money, rather than send it to the bottom and receive the lesser reward known as blood money.

The *Dolphin*'s twelve-pounders fired solid cast iron balls, the most devastating ammunition a fighting ship carried. Alternatively there was an array of projectiles aboard designed to disable a ship with great effect when fired into the ship's rigging, especially if the crew were intending on taking the vessel as a prize. The ammunition included chain-shot, which was two small cast iron balls attached by a length of chain, and bar shot, two cast iron balls joined by a sliding or solid iron bar, projectiles which spiralled through the air

The crew from an eighteenth-century frigate, armed with cutlasses, board a ship under the cover of musket fire from men positioned in the ship's fighting tops. Their purpose was to take the vessel as a prize rather than send it to the bottom of the sea.

after firing from the ship's guns, smashing into the yards and mast and cutting through the ship's rigging. This type of ammunition not only caused destructive effects to the ship; any unfortunate crewman in the path of its flight could easily have an arm or leg smashed away if not killed outright when hit by one of these lethal projectiles.

A vessel taken as a prize would be sold along with any cargo on orders from the High Court of the Admiralty. After the court took a percentage of the proceeds from the sale, the remainder would then be divided by eighths and shared between officers and the crew of the ship which had taken the prize. Three-eighths of the prize money would usually go to the captain, unless he had an area commander in which case one-third of the captain's prize would go to him. One-eighth was divided between the wardroom officers, one-eighth divided among the warrant officers and if the ship had a complement of marines aboard one-eighth would go to the lieutenant of marines. One-eighth was divided among the junior warrant and petty officers, mates and midshipmen, with the remainder divided amongst the crew, the able seamen receiving a larger share than ordinary seamen and boy sailors. Once divided the prize share out could earn a frigate captain as much as £20,000, with an ordinary seaman receiving around £100.

Two months after capturing its first prize, the *Dolphin* encountered a French privateer, the eight-gun *Ursula*, which the frigate took with hardly any resistance. However the *Dolphin* faced a much more dangerous privateer when patrolling the English Channel on a November evening in 1757. Accompanied by the frigate *Hussar*, the ships were sailing off the Channel Islands when one of the lookouts spotted a sail of an unidentified ship in the distance. In expectation of encountering a privateer which would bring both frigates a share of prize money, the *Dolphin* and the *Hussar* sailed towards the unidentified ship. With the failing light, the frigates were unable to establish the vessel's nationality and a fierce exchange of gunfire ensued.

Both frigates' gunners used all of the expertise in trying to disable the ship rather than sink it, as this large heavily armed adversary would make a magnificent prize if captured. The smaller frigates were able to out-manoeuvre the larger vessel, as both continued to fire into the ship's masts, rigging and gundecks. The ship was unwilling to yield under the onslaught, which continued for almost two hours. By the end of the engagement, the vessel had sustained so much damage that it sank below the waves with all hands.

The ship was later identified as the vastly superior French fifty-gun *L' Alcyon*.

The following year, the *Dolphin* was engaged in one of the most spectacular actions it would face during its long naval service, when coming up against Commodore Francois Thurot commanding the French forty-four-gun privateer, *Le Marechal de Belle-Isle*. Commodore Thurot, a Frenchman of Irish descent, had become an extremely successful privateer through actions carried out against British merchant shipping where in one year alone he captured sixty ships. Although the privateer was feared through his actions carried out against British commerce at sea, Commodore Thurot was a well respected ship commander, having a reputation as a man of honour.

The *Dolphin* had been ordered to Leith in Scotland, to patrol the shipping lanes of the North Sea, where privateers had been regularly attacking British merchant shipping. On 21 May 1758, a message was received at the port that a privateer had been sighted operating off the north coast of Scotland. The *Dolphin*, accompanied by the frigate *Solebay*, immediately set sail to intercept this unknown privateer. At eight o'clock in the morning on the 27 May, the *Dolphin* encountered Commodore Thurots' *Le Marechal de Belle-Isle*, sailing between Arbroath and Montrose. The *Dolphin*, out sailing the *Solebay*, was the first to clear for action making a heading towards the large privateer. Commodore Thurot, on sighting the *Dolphin*, took the naval frigate for a merchantman and made his ship ready to engage. The privateer heavily out gunned the *Dolphin*, however Captain Marlow gave the order to open fire on the Frenchman as the frigate came into range.

The *Dolphin* fought the privateer for over an hour-and-a-half, where both ships engaged each other in a ferocious exchange of gunfire. When the *Solebay* joined in the action, the *Dolphin* had suffered severe damage to its main yard and slings, forcing the frigate to fall behind to make running repairs while the *Solebay* engaged Commodore Thurot's ship. When the *Dolphin* returned to the action, the *Solebay* had also suffered a considerable amount of damage to its masts and rigging and the frigate's captain had received a seriously injury. Although both frigates suffered heavy damage, they both continued to fire upon the privateer. Commodore Thurot was unable to force either of the frigates to surrender and with his own ship taking much more punishment from the guns of the frigates than he had expected, he set a course away from the action to make his escape. At the end of the engagement the *Dolphin* and the *Solebay* reported that between them they had lost six men, with twenty-eight wounded. Although Commodore Thurot continued with his raids against British merchant shipping, he was eventually killed during a battle with British ships off the Isle of Man in February 1760.

After the *Dolphin*'s repairs had been carried out, the frigate continued on escort and patrol duties under the command of Captain Marlow until 1761, when the courageous naval captain was assigned a new posting. Captain Marlow's naval career continued to flourish after leaving the *Dolphin*, rising through the naval ranks to become an Admiral. Throughout the remainder of the Seven Years' War, the *Dolphin* carried out escort duties to the Americas and West Indies under the command of Robert Keeler, an ambitious young officer who had been promoted

The Dolphin *and* Solebay *in battle with the privateer* Le Marechal de Belle-Isle. *Both frigates sustained a considerable amount of damage during the engagement, but continued to fire on Commodore Thurot's more heavily armed ship.*

to the rank of captain in May 1761. The *Dolphin*'s duties were to protect British shipping convoys from attack by pirates and French privateers, where Captain Keeler proved himself to be an extremely competent frigate commander. Throughout its time patrolling American waters, the *Dolphin* was involved in several engagements against the French, which resulted in the capture of two privateers, the *Mars* and *Dunkerque* and the packet ship *Duc d'Aiguillon*, prizes which brought the *Dolphin*'s captain, officers and crew large rewards. At the end of the hostilities between Britain and France, the *Dolphin* returned to home waters where the officers and crew, on receiving their pay and prize money, were paid off and *Dolphin* was laid up in dock awaiting a structural survey.

On long active service, a ship in need of repair and maintenance, which could not take place at sea, would have to find a place to lay-up for the necessary work to be completed, or go to the nearest naval dockyard where a shipyard crew would be charged with carrying the required repairs. When in dock for minor maintenance and repair, the crew of the ship would remain aboard while work took place, keeping busy by cleaning and scraping the ship's bottom, to free the hull from a build up of weed and barnacles and cleaning the ship, inside and out. However, if a major refit was needed, the crew would be accommodated on a holding ship until the work was completed. After a ship had been at sea for more than ten years, the vessel would require a full survey, to determine its seaworthiness. This would mean the ship would be laid up at the end of a voyage and the crew paid off and assigned to another ship. If an officer had no other ship to go to, he would receive half-pay and wait in the hope that his services would continue to be required. After the survey of the *Dolphin* was completed, which found the ship to be sound but in need of repair, the frigate underwent a full refit at Chatham dockyard.

While the frigate was in dock at Chatham, the Admiralty were having discussions regarding effectiveness and efficiency of copper sheathing fitted to the hull of ships. These discussions led to recommendations that a ship should be found and further trials carried out. The Admiralty first experimented with copper sheathing in 1761, fitted to the hull of the frigate *Alarm*. Copper sheets were used to protect the ship's timber-built hull from wood-boring sea worms, a parasite that caused severe damage to ships' timbers below the waterline. The ship chosen for the trial was the *Dolphin*, only the second ship ever to be fitted with copper sheathing. As the yards at Chatham were unable carry out this type of work, the *Dolphin* returned to Woolwich, where the frigate remained until the fitting of the sheathing was completed at a cost of £7,975 14s.

After the successful conclusion to the Seven Years' War, British trade and colonial interest extended further out around the known world and with no wars to fight, the Admiralty turned its attention to the exploration of the Pacific Ocean and sub-continent, to further Britain's commercial interests into the southern seas. While the *Dolphin* was in dock having copper sheathing fitted, the Admiralty was planning an explorational circumnavigation of the world. With funds, ships and men readably available, the Admiralty made plans to be the first to establish a naval base in the Southern Atlantic, from where the Royal Navy would be able to patrol and control British interests in the southern oceans. Britain's interests centred upon discovering new islands and the continent *Terra Australis Incognita* – Australia – a great land-mass located in the Southern Hemisphere.

In March 1764, as the final copper sheathing was being fitted onto the *Dolphin*'s hull, Commodore John Byron arrived at Woolwich dockyard with orders to take command of the frigate. Commodore Byron, great grandfather of the poet Lord Byron, was a battle-hardened forty-two-year-old sailor who had joined the service when just a young boy. Serving as midshipman he later accompanied George Anson on his own historic circumnavigation of the globe. In April 1764, Commodore Byron received orders from the Admiralty to make the *Dolphin* ready to sail on a voyage of discovery. By June of that year the *Dolphin* was ready to sail as lead ship on an expedition to the Southern Hemisphere, accompanied by the sloop *Tamar* and the supply ship *Florida*. On leaving Woolwich, the frigate made its way down-river heading out of the Thames estuary towards the Downs, however the expedition almost came to an untimely end before it began, when the *Dolphin* ran aground in shallow water heading down the

A New Map of the WHOLE
According to $\check{y}$ latest and most Exact Obs-

In this Maps is inserted A View of $\check{y}$ General & Coasting Trade-
Winds, Monsoons or $\check{y}$ Shifting Trade-winds Note that $\check{y}$ Arrows
among $\check{y}$ Lines shew $\check{y}$ Course of those General & Coasting Winds.
and $\check{y}$ Arrows in $\check{y}$ void Spaces shew $\check{y}$ Course of $\check{y}$ Shifting Trade-
winds, and $\check{y}$ Abbreviation Sep.t &c.
Shew $\check{y}$ Times of $\check{y}$ Year when
such Winds Blow.

The GREAT
Variable Winds
Artick Circle
NORTH AMERICA
Baffin Bay
Hudson Bay
Canada
NEW FRANCE
Anian Str
California
Mexico
Mex. G.
Tro. of Cancer
los Ladrones
the Zodiack
Equinoctial Line
Hoopenn Isl.
Tro. of Capricorn
Variable Winds
New Zieland
SOUTH SEA
Fly I. Dogs I.
I. Salomon
I. S. Iuan F.
T. FIRMA
AMERICA
Brazil
Peru
Paraguay
Chili
Patagonia
R. de la Plata
Str. of Magellan
C. Horn
LaPlata
ATLANTIC
Western Ocean
ENGLAND
New England
Mary Land
Virginia
Carolina
Bermudas I.
Bahama I.
North Sea
Guinea
Antarctick Circle

WORLD with the Trade winds

ervations By H. Moll Geographer

The Signs of the Zodiack. The First 6 are Northern, the other Southern Signs

♈ Aries . March   ♌ Leo . Iuly   ♐ Sagittarius . November
♉ Taurus . April   ♍ virgo . August   ♑ Capricornus . Decemb
♊ Gemini . May   ♎ Libra . September ♒ Aquarius . Ianuary
♋ Cancer . Iune   ♏ Scorpio . October ♓ Pisces . February

139

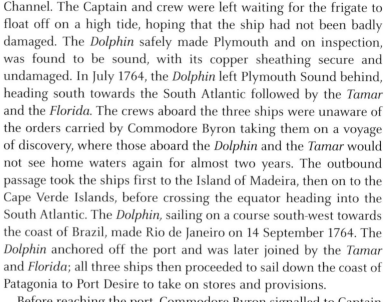

Captain of the Dolphin for the frigate's first circumnavigation of the globe, Commodore John Byron. Byron had sailed with Commodore George Anson on his own historic circumnavigation in 1740.

Channel. The Captain and crew were left waiting for the frigate to float off on a high tide, hoping that the ship had not been badly damaged. The *Dolphin* safely made Plymouth and on inspection, was found to be sound, with its copper sheathing secure and undamaged. In July 1764, the *Dolphin* left Plymouth Sound behind, heading south towards the South Atlantic followed by the *Tamar* and the *Florida*. The crews aboard the three ships were unaware of the orders carried by Commodore Byron taking them on a voyage of discovery, where those aboard the *Dolphin* and the *Tamar* would not see home waters again for almost two years. The outbound passage took the ships first to the Island of Madeira, then on to the Cape Verde Islands, before crossing the equator heading into the South Atlantic. The *Dolphin,* sailing on a course south-west towards the coast of Brazil, made Rio de Janeiro on 14 September 1764. The *Dolphin* anchored off the port and was later joined by the *Tamar* and *Florida*; all three ships then proceeded to sail down the coast of Patagonia to Port Desire to take on stores and provisions.

Before reaching the port, Commodore Byron signalled to Captain Mouatt, the commander of the *Tamar*, that he should bring the *Tamar* up with the *Dolphin* and come aboard for further orders. Commander Byron informed his officers they would be sailing on a voyage of discovery taking on a circumnavigation of the world. Any protests or objections the crew may have had when informed they would be spending the next two years of their lives at sea, were dispelled when the crew were made aware that they would all receive double pay. It was customary for Admiralty orders to be kept from all those aboard, apart from the ship's senior officers, until the ships were far out at sea in an attempt to stop crew desertions after learning of the ship's orders and the mission.

By November, the three ships were sailing off the coast of Patagonia, heading south towards Cape Blanco and Port Desire, a small fishing port claimed by the British in 1670. Although the Spanish held their own claims over the region, Admiralty ships sailing south continued to make this a port of call before sailing on towards the cold and inhospitable Antarctic waters. On 1 December 1764, before making port, the *Dolphin* was caught up in a violent storm. Commodore Byron had come to be known as 'foul-weather-Jack', due to his frequent encounters with inhospitable weather and it seemed that bad luck had followed the commodore into the South Atlantic, when the frigate almost met with disaster while battling through some of the severest weather conditions the ships had ever encountered. The ship eventually found safe anchorage off Port Desire to ride out the storm.

After a short stay at the port, the ships sailed south making for Port Famine, taking the three ships past a small group of islands sighted to the east of the mainland. The *Dolphin*, *Tamar* and *Florida* sailed into the Straits of Magellan, a waterway dividing the landmass of Patagonia to the north and Tierra del Fuego to the south, a group of volcanic islands which made up a majority of the southern tip of South America. These straits, linking the oceans of the Atlantic and Pacific, were a difficult route to navigate, due to the narrowness of the channel and the unpredictable winds and currents in the straits. However, the route was far safer for ships sailing between the Atlantic and Pacific oceans, rather than taking their chances sailing around Cape Horn, a hazardous and dangerous stretch of water where the oceans of the Pacific and Atlantic met, resulting in huge waves, strong currents, gale force winds and all types of inhospitable weather conditions, where rain, sleet and snow made visibility almost impossible, increasing the chances of a ship colliding with submerged icebergs.

On 29 December 1764, the ships anchored at Port Famine where the *Dolphin* and *Tamar* loaded aboard the provisions from the store

The Dolphin *and the* Tamar *caught in a storm off the coast of Patagonia in 1764.*

ship *Florida*, which then sailed back home to England. Commodore Byron issued orders for the *Dolphin* and the *Tamar* to make sail on 4 January 1765. However, instead of making a heading westward through the straits, the ships sailed eastwards, out into the South Atlantic towards a group of islands off the mainland.

On arrival the *Dolphin* and the *Tamar* dropped anchor in the natural harbour of a small island to the north-west of the group. Parties from the ships were put ashore to explore the island, which Commodore Byron claimed on behalf of King George III, naming

The southern tip of South America, showing the Straits of Magellan, a much safer passage from the Atlantic into the Pacific, than chancing sailing around Cape Horn where the weather was so inhospitable that many ships attempting this passage were either forced to turn back, or were lost with all hands.

the harbour, Port Egmont. These islands had first been discovered in the early 1500s, but no sovereign nations had ever laid a claim to them. Commodore Byron sailed around the islands claiming the whole group on behalf of the King, unaware that the French had already established a small colony on an island to the east. This act resulted in years of conflicting claims and counter claims between the French, British and also by the Spanish, after they had taken the French colonial port in 1767. This resulted in the eviction of a colony of British settlers from the islands in 1770, when five Spanish warships arrived with a small army of soldiers, an act of aggression that almost brought England and Spain to the brink of war. After a treaty was signed between the two nations, the British settlers were allowed to return, however neither Britain nor Spain were willing the give up a claim over the islands, which Britain named the Falklands and the Spanish the Malvinas the sovereignty of which became an issue of contention ever since first claimed by Commodore Byron during his voyage of exploration. On leaving the Falklands, the *Dolphin* and the *Tamar* returned to Port Famine before heading west along the Straits of Magellan, sailing out into the Pacific Ocean on 9 April 1767.

Commodore Byron had sailed from England with instructions from the Admiralty to first make for New Albion, on the west coast of North America, first discovered by Drake during his own circumnavigation of the globe, then to go in search of the elusive Northwest Passage, a sea route believed to exist between the North Atlantic and North Pacific. If Commodore Byron was unsuccessful, his orders were then to return to England by way of the East Indies. However Commodore Byron chose to sail west in search of a group of islands discovered by Spanish navigator Alvaro Mendaña in 1568 while he was searching for Australia, which he had named Islas Salomon.

Eighteen days after leaving the Magellan Straits, the ships made the island of Masa Fuero, part of the Juan Fernández archipelago, 400 miles off the coast of Chile, where Commodore Byron made Captain Mouatt the commander of the *Dolphin*, acting as post captain under him. The ships sailed west, then north-west through a vast expanse of uncharted water. In June 1765, two islands were spotted by lookouts on the *Tamar* and running low of rations, the ships attempted to land at the islands. Unable to locate a safe anchorage, the ships sailed on until reaching the island of Takaroa, where both ships came to anchor off-shore. The ships' boats were launched and a party of men rowed to shore in search of provisions. The crew's attempt to land was hampered by the island's natives, who began to attack the boats as they came into shore. Desperate for provisions the boats crew fought off the islanders and took aboard whatever they were able to find on the island, which included coconuts and a large quantity of Scurvy-grass, an herbaceous plant used to help relieve the effects of scurvy.

After the confrontation with the inhospitable South Seas islanders, the *Dolphin* and the *Tamar* raised anchor sailing further west, discovering several clusters of small islands on route, which Captain Cook would later name the Society Islands during his own voyage south in 1769. The *Dolphin* and the *Tamar* continued on a course taking both vessels close to the undiscovered island of Tahiti. Unable to locate the elusive and legendary Solomon Islands, charted on a highly decorated nautical map in the seventeenth-century marine atlas, *Neptune François*, containing the most accurate charts of the time, Commodore Byron gave up on his search deciding the islands did not exist and set a course northwards, towards the Northern Marianas Islands, east of the Philippine Sea. Arriving at the island of Tinian on 30 July 1765, the ships remained at anchor off the island for almost three months while those aboard the *Dolphin* and the *Tamar*, who were suffering from scurvy, were treated with a tonic made from Scurvy-grass, which was rich in Vitamin C.

Once a majority of the crew had recovered from suffering from this dreaded ailment, which killed more British sailors than were lost in battle during the eighteenth century, Commodore Byron gave orders for the ships to make sail south-west, towards the Philippines and into more familiar waters. The *Dolphin* and its companion *Tamar* had now sailed over half-way around the globe as the vessels sailed south-west into the Java Sea making for Batavia, a Dutch colony on

The crews of the Tamar and the Dolphin taking on provisions at a Pacific island which included fresh water, a variety of the island's wildlife and Scurvy-grass, used to relieve the effects of scurvy.

the north-west coast of Java, Indonesia.

The remainder of the voyage was uneventful and with Commodore Byron eager to return home as soon as possible, both the *Dolphin* and the *Tamar* made good progress on the final stretch of the voyage. The ships sailed westward through the Indian Ocean around the Cape of Good Hope and into the Atlantic, arriving off the Downs in May 1766, to complete the fastest circumnavigation of the globe ever recorded, which had taken less than two years to complete. On the *Dolphin*'s return to Deptford dockyard, the frigate was found to be in excellent condition following the record-breaking voyage around the world. Commodore Byron had written in his journal, while in Port Famine during the expedition, that in his opinion 'copper bottoms were the finest invention in the world'. This gave good reason for further experiments to be carried out to investigate the benefits of sheathing a ships bottom in copper, however the Admiralty were slow in implementing the fitting out of all naval ships with copper bottoms, which did not become standard practice until the late 1700s.

The *Dolphin* remained docked at Deptford during the summer of 1766, where a further inspection carried out declared the vessel fit to continue service. The frigate's bottom was then re-clad with new copper sheathing and the *Dolphin* was ready for sea once again. A new commander was appointed to the frigate; Captain Samuel

Wallis, a Cornishman born to gentry who owned estates near Camelford. Captain Wallis had joined the navy as a midshipman and saw action during the 1744 and 1749 wars with France, after which he was promoted through the ranks to captain, taking command of his own ship in 1756. Captain Wallis had previously commanded the sixty-gun *Prince of Orange*, deployed in the Channel Fleet up until the Treaty of Paris was signed in February 1763, which concluded the Seven Years' War. The Admiralty recalled Captain Wallis into active service with secret orders to discover lands and islands situated in the furthest extremities of the southern hemisphere between Cape Horn and the Aotearoa, now New Zealand, to investigate any beneficial commercial opportunities which may exist in these remote regions and to search for a southerly trade route to the lucrative East Indies.

Sailing from Plymouth in August 1766, the *Dolphin* was accompanied on the voyage by the store-ship *Prince Frederick* and the sloop *Swallow*, commanded by Captain Philip Carteret who had sailed as lieutenant under Commodore John Byron, on the *Dolphin*'s first circumnavigation of the globe. Captain Wallis knew that the *Dolphin* was up to the task of a second circumnavigation; however he had less confidence in the *Swallow*, which he considered far from ship-shape and not suitable for such a voyage. Both ships' commanders did not get along and Wallis kept his orders secret from Captain Carteret until some three weeks out to sea, with the captain of the *Swallow* believing they were heading for the Falkland Islands to re-provision the settlement at Port Egmont.

The *Swallow* was not the fastest of sailing vessels but was a dependable little ship, although its commander thought the posting, along with the ship under his command, a liability that would hold him back from his expected advancement through the ranks. The three ships made slow passage southwards, down through the Atlantic towards the Strait of Magellan, where they did not arrive until mid-December 1766. Wallis then ordered the *Swallow* to act as pilot heading for Port Famine which took ten sailing days. Provisions were loaded aboard the *Dolphin* and *Swallow* and after off-loading supplies from the *Prince Frederick*, the storeship was ordered to make for the Falkland Islands.

An arduous passage through the Magellan Straights followed, where both vessels were in constant danger of shipwreck as they navigated their way through this most inhospitable stretch of water. On reaching Cape Pilar, the *Dolphin*'s sails were let out to swiftly take the ship out into the Pacific during the night, with the *Swallow*

Samuel Wallace, who commanded the Dolphin *on the frigate's second circumnavigation around the globe, was recalled into active service after the end of the Seven Years' War.*

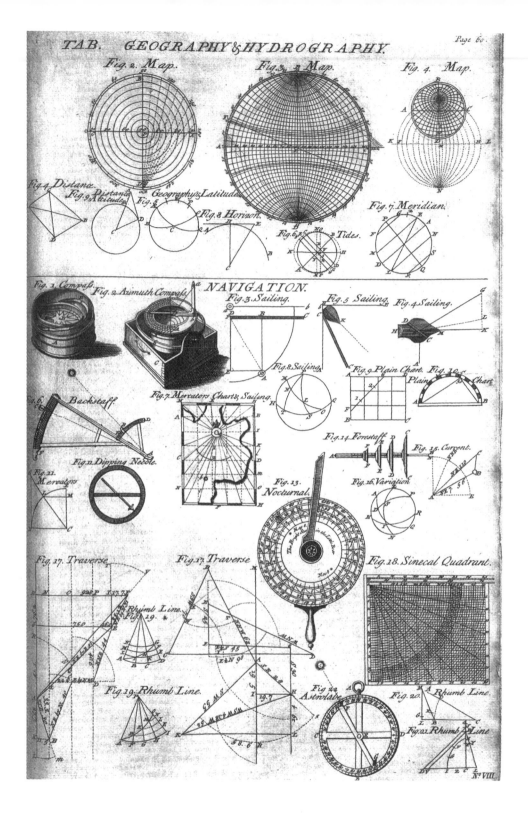

Fig. 2. Map.

Fig. 3. a Map.

Fig. 4. Map.

Fig. 4. Distance.

Fig. 9. Altitude.

Geography & Latitude.

Fig. 5.

Fig. 8. Horizon.

Fig. 6. Tides.

Fig. 7. Meridian.

NAVIGATION.

Fig. 1. Compass.

Fig. 2. Azimuth Compass.

Fig. 3. Sailing.

Fig. 5. Sailing.

Fig. 4. Sailing.

Fig. 8. Sailing.

Fig. 9. Plain Chart.

Fig. 10. Plain Chart.

Fig. 6. Backstaff.

Fig. 7. Mercators Charts, Sailing.

Fig. 11. Dipping Needle.

Fig. 14. Forestaff.

Fig. 15. Current.

Fig. 21. Mercator.

Fig. 16. Variation.

Fig. 13. Nocturnal.

Fig. 17. Traverse.

Fig. 17. Traverse.

Fig. 18. Sinecal Quadrant.

Rhumb Line.
Fig. 19.

Fig. 19. Rhumb Line.

Fig. 12. Astrolabe.

Fig. 20. Rhumb Line.

Fig. 21. Rhumb Line.

Nº VIII.

expected to follow on the same course. However by daybreak, the lookouts aboard the *Dolphin* had lost sight of the sloop and the frigate sailed on alone.

While the *Dolphin* was forced northwards by the north-west winds, Captain Carteret sailed his on his own course hoping to make the nearest landfall to take on provisions and supplies. After an unsuccessful attempt to land at Spanish occupied Juan Fernández Islands and then the Island of Más Afuera, off the west coast of Chile, the *Swallow* sailed on westwards with Captain Carteret promising a bottle of brandy to the first man aboard to sight land. This honour was awarded to a fifteen-year-old midshipman named Robert Pitcairn, who was the first to spot an isolated island on the horizon. The island was named after him and Pitcairn Island later became home to the descendants of the *Bounty* mutineers. The *Swallow* continued on its voyage, with no further contact or sight of the *Dolphin*, returning to England by March 1769.

Captain Wallis sailed on for two months after losing sight of the *Swallow,* reaching a group of islands which made up the Tuamotu Archipelago, where the islanders supplied the ship with fresh provisions and water. On 18 June 1767, the *Dolphin* was sailing on a heading west-north-west when a much larger island was sighted in the distance. Captain Wallis had discovered the Polynesian island of Otaheite, Tahiti. Sailing on towards the island, the *Dolphin* hove to as darkness fell, with the island still some distance ahead. At 2.00 a.m. the following day, the ship made sail in the early morning light, heading towards the island, some five leagues distant.

As the frigate came close to the island, a thick fog bank set in, forcing the ship's crew to take down sail to slow the frigate's progress in these uncharted waters. When the fog cleared, the crew were astonished to find the *Dolphin* surrounded by over a hundred canoes, manned by the island's natives. At first, the crew of the *Dolphin* were hesitant and suspicious of the natives' intent, then after showing the islanders trinkets and gifts while they continued to paddle around the ship in their canoes, the crew tentatively invited them aboard. Eventually the islanders made their own signs of friendship and one of their members began waving a branch of a palm tree and making a long speech, which Captain Wallis believed to be a message of welcome.

One young islander came aboard the ship by climbing athletically up the mizzen chains and jumped out of the shrouds onto the top of the awning. Encouraged by the crew to come down, he was offered gifts which at first he refused, until other islanders came

Opposite: *Table of geography, hydrography and navigation from the* Cyclopaedia of Arts and Sciences, *published by Ephraim Chambers in 1728. Ever since the medieval period, navigation was considered one of the seven mechanical arts, the other six included blacksmithing, agriculture, hunting, medicine, weaving and war. The understanding of navigation and hydrography, the knowledge of measuring water depths and the movement of tides and currents, was essential when sailing the oceans of the globe. The British Royal Navy were at the forefront of charting and surveying the seas and oceans around the world, where naval vessels made extensive navigational and hydrographical records during voyages.*

aboard and ceremonially threw down palm tree branches upon the ship's deck, after which the islander graciously accepted the gifts offered.

Finding that the islanders appeared to be friendly, Wallis decided to search for a safe place to anchor and sailed the frigate into a large open bay to the north of the island. On sailing into the bay the frigate hit a submerged ridge towards the north of the mouth of the bay, which would forever be marked on sailing charts as 'Dolphin's Bank'. Undamaged in the collision, the ship's cutter was launched to take soundings before the frigate proceeded any further. As soon as the cutter made its way into the bay, the boat was surrounded by the islander's canoes, and Captain Wallis became extremely concerned for the safety of his men. Sending a signal for the boat to return, suspecting that his men may come under attack at any moment, Wallis gave orders to fire the ship's nine-pounder above the heads of the islanders to serve as a warning.

As the cutter changed course making its way back towards the *Dolphin*, the canoes began surrounding the boat in an attempt block the boat's course, with one canoe ramming into the cutter. Although startled by the firing of the ship's gun, islanders armed with war clubs attempted to board the cutter. One of the officers aboard the cutter opened fire with a musket full of buckshot, wounding one of the islanders in the shoulder and hitting another who fell dead into the water. The gunfire frightened away the islanders who paddled their canoes back to shore and the cutter sailed safely away.

The soundings found the bay to have a sandy bottom, which was around eight to sixteen fathoms deep, making the bay a safe place for anchorage. Wallis later named the bay Matavai, Port Royal Harbour. Although now safely at anchor, the frigate continued to came under further attack from the islanders during the first few days after the ship sailed into in the bay. Then a hostile force of islanders approached the *Dolphin* in large war canoes, one coming close enough to the frigate that the islanders could hurl stones and rocks at the ship and crew. The *Dolphin*'s crew replied by firing the ship's guns, which were loaded with grapeshot. One of the shots hit its target cutting the canoe in two. The firepower from the *Dolphin* frightened off the attacking warriors who paddled their canoes back to shore. The following day, Captain Wallis sent a party of men ashore to plant the British flag, claiming the island in the name of King George III. Two days later, another fleet of war canoes made out from the shore in an attempt to attack the *Dolphin* and Captain Wallis once again ordered the gun crew to open fire on the canoes. When the islanders retreated, taking up a position on a hill overlooking the bay, the *Dolphin*'s gun crew then targeted the hill and opened fire, killing a number of islanders and injuring many others. After these confrontations, Captain Wallis put his carpenters ashore to cut the islanders' canoes in half in an attempt to stop the attacks on the frigate.

The Otaheite islanders eventually conceded to the superior gun power of the frigate and a peaceful relationship grew. After gaining each other's trust it was not long before trading was taking place between the *Dolphin*'s crew and islanders, who wanted woven cloth and anything made of iron, in exchange for provisions of

fruit, vegetables, poultry and pigs. Many of the crew from the ship succumbed to the seductive charms and sexual favours offered by the island's beautiful dark haired young women, where in exchange for the delights on offer, the crew began stealing anything from the ship made of iron, even pulling the iron nails out from the ship's planking, which the islanders used to make fishing hooks. After Captain Wallis became aware of these thefts taking place, he issued orders that all crew would remain aboard ship until the thieves were discovered and punished, reminding the crew of the regulations for conduct while going ashore. Captain Wallis was then required to read out the articles of war to his crew, after the corporal of marines struck the master at arms after the marine had deserted his duties attempting to get ashore to partake in the pleasures available.

Once a degree of discipline was restored aboard ship, which Captain Wallis and his offices found difficult to maintain throughout the five week stay, further explorations of the island were carried out to locate provisions. The temptations of this island paradise not only caused problems for the captain of the *Dolphin* in maintaining discipline amongst his officers and men, the delights on offer also contributed to the breakdown in order for captains of ships which followed. Captain Cook had trouble maintaining discipline aboard the *Endeavour* when putting into the island in 1769 and the infamous Captain Bligh lost command of the *Bounty*, when his crew mutinied after setting sail from the island in 1789.

Above: *The* Dolphin *opens fire on the islander's canoes which began attacking the frigate after the ship came to anchor in Port Royal Harbour, named in honour of King George III.*

Below: *King George III. Captain Wallis claimed the island of Otaheite in the name of the King of England in 1767.*

After the initial hostilities, the islanders had become extremely friendly and hospitable, with many of the island's chieftains coming aboard the *Dolphin* to visit Captain Wallis. When Captain Wallis, his first lieutenant and the purser were suffering from a feverish illness, the ship's gunner brought aboard a tall, majestic woman, who Captain Wallis took to be of great importance by the way the islanders were so respective of her. After pleasantries were exchanged, Captain Wallis came to the conclusion that he was in the presence of the Queen of Otaheite.

Captain Wallis presented the Queen with gifts of beads, a looking glass and a long blue mantle, which he placed over her head and

The beautiful Polynesian women the crew of the Dolphin *encountered were often described or depicted as parading around fully or semi-naked, which was readily interpreted as young woman having strong stirrings of sexual desire. However it was customary for the young woman of Tahiti to give new arrivals to the islands a gift of cloth, unwound from the clothes they wore, a tiputa, on their upper bodies. The Europeans who encountered this ceremonial welcome, where the young woman revealed their breasts in front of them, considered this be an open invitation for sexual encounters. There is no doubt that liaison between ships' crews and the island's alluring young women took place with the islander's full consent, in exchange for gifts on offer.*

fastened with ribbons. The Queen of Otaheite pointed towards shore inviting Captain Wallis, his first-lieutenant and the purser to accompany her onto the island. The next morning Captain Wallis and his two officers were taken ashore by the islanders, the first occasion the *Dolphin's* commander had been onto the island since arriving and all three men were carried to a large open sided thatched roofed house. Once taken inside Captain Wallis and his officers received treatment from four young native women who massaged the officer's lower legs and feet, which Captain Wallis found to be extremely beneficial to his health.

Before the *Dolphin* departed from the island, Captain Wallis and his officers were invited by the Queen to a ceremonial gathering, where they were presented with decorative feathered headdresses, several unusual woven grass mats and platted 'hau' headbands, made from the Queen's own hair. The following day after Captain Wallis and his officers had returned to the ship, the islanders provided the crew with large quantities of exotic fruits and over twenty live hogs for the voyage home.

On the morning of 27 July 1767, with Captain Wallis about to give the order to make ready for sail, a flotilla of canoes surrounded the *Dolphin* before the frigate was able to weigh anchor. A large double canoe then came up upon the frigate with the Queen of Otaheite aboard. Invited aboard the frigate, the Queen, distraught and weeping uncontrollably, expressed great sorrow at the departure of the *Dolphin* and its crew. As a light breeze came up the order was given to raise anchor and make sail and the Queen embraced the ship's commander and officers before returning with her attendants to the canoe. As the wind caught in the *Dolphin*'s sails the canoe with the Queen standing in the bow, still weeping, came alongside the frigate's port gunroom where Captain Wallis handed down further gifts which he thought might be of use. Although the gifts were accepted, the *Dolphin*'s commander could see that the Queen hardly took any notice of them, because of her grief and her sorrow.

Captain Wallis wrote in his journal

'...our Indian friends and particularly the queen, once more bade us farewell, with such tenderness of affection and grief, as filled both my heart and my eyes ... the benefit that we received while we lay off this island, with respect to the health of the ship's company, was beyond our most sanguine expectations, for we had not now an invalid on board, except the two Lieutenants and myself and we were recovering, though still in a very feeble condition'.

During the time *Dolphin* was anchored in the bay, Captain Wallis had compiled extensive written accounts and reports of Otaheite, the islanders and their culture, which included a series of detailed colourful drawings of flying fish, the Queen's long house and the large green-skinned breadfruit plant, the staple food of Pacific islanders. These breadfruits, rich in carbohydrates, were considered an ideal source of cheap, high-energy food for feeding to British slaves. After their discovery, Captain Bligh was sent on a mission to Tahiti in 1787, on the *Bounty* to gather up breadfruit cuttings for transportation to the British slave colonies for cultivation.

Although Captain Wallis claimed Otaheite, Tahiti, on behalf the British crown, the following year French explorer Louis Bougainville landed, claiming the island on behalf of France. In April 1769, Captain James Cook set up camp on the island under secret orders to view the transit of Venus. Captain Cook returned in 1773, then later in 1777, finding this once tranquil paradise had changed drastically. There had been a dramatic fall in the island's population and the Tahitians were now in all-out war with other Polynesian islanders. There was a common belief in Western Europe that acts of cannibalism were being carried out throughout Polynesia, which many believed to be the cause for the dramatic fall in the island's population. Although human and animal sacrifices did take place on Tahiti during the late 1700s, which Captain Cook had witnessed when visiting the island in 1773, Captain Wallis had not seen or

Breadfruit plant illustrated by John Frederick Miller (1759-1796), an artist who produced paintings from sketches made during voyages of exploration.

heard of any cannibalism taking place on Tahiti. The most likely reason for the belief that cannibalism took place on remote islands, came through sailors returning from long voyages deliberately spreading these stories because this is what God-fearing European Christians wanted to hear about heathen savages living in far off

Captain Bligh's ship the Bounty, *drawn by S. Drée. In 1787 the* Bounty *was purchased by the Royal Navy and refitted out at Deptford for a voyage to Tahiti to load cuttings of the breadfruit plant for transportation to Britain's slave colonies. However mutiny broke out aboard ship soon after departing Tahiti. The men were rebelling against what they perceived as harsh treatment by Captain Bligh during the voyage. Bligh was set adrift in the ship's launch along with any crew who remained loyal to him. Bligh miraculously navigated almost 4,000 miles to safety, while the mutineers landed at Pitcairn Island where they set fire to the* Bounty *to avoid detection and prevent any of the mutineers deserting.*

distant lands. The main cause for the fall in the island's population came from decease and infection which included smallpox, typhus and syphilis all spread by the crews of visiting ships. When the *Dolphin* first arrived at Tahiti the population was around 160,000, however when the *Bounty* had sailed away from the island in 1789, the population had dropped to a mere 16,000.

Wallis would later write,

'It is certain that none of our people contracted the venereal disease here and therefore, as they had free commerce with great

A Ju-ju house where ceremonial sacrifices were believed to take place and the flesh of the victims eaten. The stories of these rituals were based on supposition, as written accounts recorded journals and periodicals of the day were sensationalised by the authors.

numbers of the women, there is the greatest probability that it was not then known in the country. It was, however, found here by Captain Cook, in the *Endeavour* and as no European vessel is known to have visited this island before Captain Cook's arrival, but the *Dolphin* and the *Boudese* and *Etoile*, commanded by M. Bougainville, the reproach of having contaminated with that dreadful pest a race of happy people to whom its miseries had till then been unknown must either be due to him or me, to England or to France; and I think myself happy to be able to exculpate myself and my country beyond the possibility of doubt'.

The *Dolphin* sailed for home, following a similar course taken by Captain Byron, westwards towards the Solomon Islands and then into the Philippine Sea. Captain Wallis continued to suffer from the effects of his illness, with many of his crew also stricken down with fevers, scurvy and dysentery. The *Dolphin*'s captain tried to maintain the health of his crew by using a three-shift rotation, which gave his crew more time to rest. He also ordered the ship to be kept clean and well aired and ensured the ship was provisioned with fresh fruit and vegetables. Captain Cook later adopted the ideas of Captain Wallis for his own voyages of exploration and discovery aboard the *Endeavour*.

By the time the frigate reached the islands of Indonesia, several of those suffering from their illnesses had died. Wallis wrote in his log on route to the Cape,

'Every day we have numbers of people taken ill of fevers and fluxes and they all seem greatly dejected. The air is damp and unwholesome. The ship is kept very clean and every possible assistance given to the sick, yet the number increases... Sick list forty two...thirty can scarcely crawl, gave surgeon 20lb of soap to wash sick men's clothes'.

As the *Dolphin* sailed on into the Atlantic, the frigate was also suffering from the rigours of the voyage. The frigate's sails were in constant need of repair and rats, which infested the ship, were eating through all of the stores and provisions. On 20 May 1768, the stricken ship finally sailed into Plymouth to complete a second circumnavigation of the globe. There was no doubt this had been a dangerous and hazardous voyage of exploration, which had taken officers and crew away from their homes and loved ones for almost three years. Seven of the ship's crew had lost their lives during the voyage and many others returned in an extremely poor state of health. When the *Dolphin's* commander, officers and crew were paid off, one of the crew handed a petition to Captain Wallis as he was leaving the ship which read,

'Sir, we should not have dared to have made this bold with you, had we not been encouraged by the Humane and generous treatment we have so often experienced since we have had the happiness to be commanded by you. And thinks it our duty to return you our most sincere thanks for the many instances of that generous treatment we

have had from you. And as you are the only Prop we have to depend on hopes that this address will not be without success. We humbly beg that you may recommend us to their Lordships favor as it is certain that thro your goodness in so doing must depend our good or bad fortunes and as we came out in a state of uncertainty, makes us thus bold to solicit you in our behalf. And may you live long and happy to be a service as well as an Honour to your Country are the Prayers of Sir Your Most Obedient and most humble Servants - The Dolphins.'

It is certain that the *Dolphin's* crew, who although experiencing some of the harshest and severest conditions during their long voyage around the world, were all in agreement that Captain Wallis had shown himself throughout to be an excellent and honourable commander.

The Admiralty considered the *Dolphin's* voyage to be a great success and the recorded details and navigational findings made by Captain Wallis and his officers during the voyage were used extensively in preparation for Captain Cook's voyage of exploration and several members of the *Dolphin's* crew later signed up to sail with Captain Cook on the *Endeavour*. Captain Wallis continued to suffer from his illness for some time after his return, leaving naval service on half-pay. He was later recalled to duty for a short period during 1770, when there had been a threat of war between Britain and Spain. Captain Wallis was appointed Commissioner of the Admiralty in 1780 and after his death in 1795, his circumnavigation and voyage of discovery aboard the *Dolphin* was commemorated on a memorial erected in Truro Cathedral.

The *Dolphin*, now in its sixteenth year of naval service required a complete survey after the voyage and the frigate was despatched to the dockyards at Deptford. The copper sheathing was removed from *Dolphin*, to allow for a full survey to take place, after which, the frigate remained in dock for two years where a complete overhaul and refit was carried out. In April 1770, Captain Digby Dent, a career officer with a long Royal Naval family pedigree, was appointed the *Dolphin*'s new commander. Once re-sheathed in copper the frigate was ready for commissioning in June of that year. Sailing under the command of Captain Dent, the frigate's duties were to patrol and protect British trading interests in the waters of the mid-Atlantic, between Africa and South America. Towards the end of 1771 the *Dolphin* received orders to sail for the East Indies, under the command of Captain Henry Lloyd, for further patrol and escort duties. The command of the ship later transferred over to Captain Gideon Johnstone who had recently earned a promotion in June 1772. Captain Johnstone remained in command of the frigate for three years while stationed in Madras and Calcutta, patrolling the Indian Ocean to ensure British interests were secure in the East Indies. However this was not the most desirable of postings for officers or crew; the climate was extremely inhospitable and with the overcrowded and cramped living conditions aboard ship, there was always the potential for disease breaking out aboard. The inhospitable conditions the crews faced, resulted in many instances of desertion from Royal Naval ships, where men were attracted by better pay and better prospects serving aboard an East Indiaman or by joining the private armies of Indian princes. In February 1774, while the *Dolphin* was at anchor in Calcutta, three of the frigate's crew who attempted to dessert were given fifty lashes each under the orders of Captain Johnstone, a punishment carried out in front of the rest of the crew, to act as a warning to those who also had a desire to try to make their escape.

The *Dolphin* remained in the Indian Ocean for another eighteen months under the command of Captain John Clarke. However, the *Dolphin*'s captain passed away in November 1775 and the frigate's first-lieutenant, James Pigot, was officially appointed commander in February 1776. The *Dolphin* had now been in service for twenty-five years and was beginning to show its age where water continuously leaked in through its planking, causing extremely unpleasant sailing conditions for officers and crew aboard, especially during severe weather conditions and torrential downfalls of rain during the monsoons.

After just over a year in command of the *Dolphin*, Captain Pigot received orders to make the frigate ready to sail for England. In March 1776, before the frigate's departure from Bombay, Captain Pigot received orders to take aboard a very sick young midshipman who had been discharged from the frigate *Seahorse* through illness. Suffering a serious bought of malaria, which was a life threatening disease at the time, a young Horatio Nelson was taken aboard and given berth space on the *Dolphin*, for transportation home to England. Nelson spent a majority of his time on the frigate recuperating from his illness, finding the voyage home a harrowing and depressing experience. Towards the final part of the voyage, he had recovered sufficiently, to be able to carry out some light duties aboard. Although the condition of the ship was in as poor a state as Nelson's own health, the midshipman was in praise of the frigate, finding the *Dolphin* to be an extremely swift sailing vessel. The *Dolphin* arrived off Spithead towards the end of August 1776 and then proceeded on to Woolwich where the frigate was paid off on 24 September 1776. After his return, Horatio Nelson remarked that the kindness shown to him by the *Dolphin's* commander Captain James Pigot, had saved his life.

Nelson's saviour Captain Pigot went on to command one of the new type of fifth-rate frigates, rising through the ranks to reach the position of Admiral by 1802. The young Nelson's future is well documented, however if it had not been for the *Dolphin's* intervention in bringing Nelson back home from the East Indies and allowing him time to recover from his life threatening illness, then British Naval history, perhaps British history, could have turned out very differently.

Captain Horatio Nelson 1782. John Rigaud. The young midshipman, after returning from the East Indies aboard the Dolphin, *was promoted to fourth lieutenant and assigned to the* Worcester *for convoy duties in the Channel. Two years later Nelson was appointed commander of the brig* Badger *and at twenty-four years old he was appointed captain of the frigate* Albemarle.

The *Dolphin* was laid up at Woolwich where Master Shipwright, Philip Stephens, made a request for an inspection to be carried out on the frigate to obtain approval for refitting the ship for further sea duties. A full survey of the frigate was required before any decision could be made on the ship's suitability for repair and refit. When the copper sheathing was removed, the *Dolphin's* timbers were found to be in an extremely poor condition and were rotting away inside and out. A survey by the Woolwich Offices, completed in December 1776, reported that due to the frigate's extremely poor condition they recommended the *Dolphin* be taken apart and rebuilt.

Towards the latter part of the eighteenth century, the Admiralty were in favour of building larger fifth-rate frigates as replacements for smaller sixth-rate frigates which were considered too small for the duties expected of them. With the *Dolphin* laid up at Woolwich throughout the Christmas period and into the New Year, the Admiralty made the decision to decommission the frigate and take it apart, not for re-building, but for breaking up. The Admiralty now considered that the frigate was no longer fit for purpose and without any further formalities the breakers moved in and the *Dolphin* was broken up at Woolwich on 22 January 1777. Once the frigate was taken to pieces, all of the rotten timbers were cut out and disposed of, however with British oak becoming scarce, any remaining timbers in good condition were re-used in the construction and repair of other ships, or were sold off to be used in building construction and furniture making. After carrying out twenty-five years of active service in times of war, peace and exploration, sailing throughout all of the seas and oceans around the world, the breaking up of the *Dolphin* was an unfitting end for this historic ship.

Dockyard workers take apart the Dolphin *at Woolwich in 1777.*

And all I ask is a tall ship and a star to steer her by.

Sailing Vessel Tenacious. *Image courtesy of Tallshipstock.com.*

After the Millennium celebrations in the year 2000, with the world heritage site of Greenwich at the centre of these historic festivities, time moved forward into a twenty-first century where future voyages of exploration would be to the stars and the age of sail was consigned to the pages of history, along with the British shipbuilding industry. Any opportunities to go to sea on a fully rigged British-built tall ship have now become a very rare and unique experience.

When the last of the Deptford and Woolwich wooden-built naval ships rolled down the slipways, fighting vessels were beginning to be built using new age shipbuilding technologies, constructed in iron and powered by coal-fired steam engines. The East India Company, once the most powerful trading company in the world, had been dissolved by parliament in 1874, resulting in many of the surviving East Indiamen taking to shipping freight and passengers under private ownership, before they were surpassed by faster clippers and windjammers, which in turn gave way to larger iron-built steam freighters and cargo vessels, bringing an end to the days of ocean going working sailing ships. The East India Company was resurrected in 2010 by Indian entrepreneur Sanjiv Mehta, after buying the company registration from UK private investors in 2005. Trading as a consumer brand

Steam surpasses sail; the Royal Squadron leaves Woolwich in September 1845, with the Royal Yacht, the paddle steamer the Victoria & Albert, passing a sailing ship firing a royal salute. By the late 1800s, steam-powered vessels gradually began to replace sail and with the Thames beginning to silt up these larger iron-built steamships were becoming increasingly difficult to launch from the yards along the Thames.

the East India Company opened a luxury food and gift store on Conduit Street, off Regent Street in London, selling fine gourmet foods, teas, coffees, speciality sugars, chocolates and fine wines, which represent the Company's mercantile traditions and the exotic

The new East India Company premises can now be found on Conduit Street, off Regent Street, London. Although no longer a powerful trading company, exotic goods can be purchased from the store which carries the historic name.

The original East India Company House, which stood on Leadenhall Street, London, was demolished in 1862 and new premises for Lloyd's of London were built upon the site in 1925. The latest ultra modern steel and concrete building, designed by Richard Rogers & Partners, was commissioned in 1979.

cultures from around the globe where the Company once traded, however most of the goods on sale are now made in Britain, with the teas, coffees and spices used in the goods produced, shipped in from the Far East on huge container vessels.

After both the Royal Dockyards at Deptford and Woolwich closed, naval shipbuilding continued to survive north of River Thames up until the mid-1900s at the Thames Iron Works and Blackwall. When the last of these East London yards closed down, the Thames shipbuilding industry finally came to an end. The

yards at Portsmouth, the navy's first Royal Dockyard and the yards at Chatham, on the river Medway, continued on the traditions of building British naval warships, while Britain's merchant shipbuilding industry had by then become well established in the north-east of England, Scotland and Northern Ireland.

Unless you are a member of a yacht club or have limitless amounts of funds available to either buy your own sailing vessel or pay a fee to crew a tall ship, the chances of experiencing what life was like at sea, hauling rope, setting sail, raising canvas, climbing rigging and sailing for days on end without any sight of land, are now extremely rare. Even in the Royal Navy there is no longer a need for recruits to have any knowledge of taking to sea under sail, or any requirement to take up the opportunities the Royal Navy offer to get involved in sailing the old fashioned way. An acquaintance and family friend who served in the Royal Navy for

The Blackwall shipyards finally closed in 1980 and the dockyards beyond the riverside gated entrance were redeveloped. Some of the remaining warehouses were converted and new modern buildings were erected for use as offices, apartments, restaurants and leisure facilities.

more than twenty years making voyages aboard warships across the oceans around the world, has never been out on the water in a ship or boat powered by the wind.

Although there are many youth sail training opportunities available offering youngsters a chance try out some square rig sailing with organisations such as the Sail Training Association and ISAF Youth Sailing, opportunities for someone of my own age who has an urge to go to sea and experience life under sail on a square rigger, are few and far between. A majority of those available, come as an adventure sailing experience, which can cost you an arm and a leg, a price which many a true ancient mariner paid in reality during a lifetime at sea working and fighting under sail.

Taking a voyage on a tall ship had always been an ambition, especially as many of my own family members had been involved in the maritime industry since the 1800s. While compiling this publication, I wanted to find out what life was like working aboard a sailing ship, although I didn't want this experience to be just a holiday aboard, with the ship's professional crew carrying out all the hard manual work, with novice fare paying passengers sipping cocktails on deck and occasionally pulling on a few ropes. Searching through the available sailing adventures advertised, I found they were all extremely expensive, with few suiting my needs. While discussing my publication with

Ship's stern name plate, displaying the place where the vessel was built and launched.

a work colleague, a former resident of Greenwich himself, he told me about a sailing organisation, the Jubilee Sailing Trust, which provides opportunities for people to crew a square rigged ship while helping to support people with sensory and physical disabilities who also have a yearning to take to sea under sail. The Jubilee Sailing Trust, a registered charity, was founded to make it possible for people of all physical abilities to sail a tall ship on as near equal terms as possible. The trust operates two square rigged sailing vessels, the *Lord Nelson* and the *Tenacious*, which

Below left: *Looking aft of the* Tenacious *towards the ship's bridge area, accessed by steps and a lift for wheelchair users.*

Below right: *All square sails set on the* Tenacious *as wind picks up.*

are the only ships of their kind in the world designed and built specifically to enable people with various sensory and physical disabilities to sail as full members of the ship's crew, who are buddied up with an able-bodied member of the crew who sign up to help and assist them during the voyage.

Having been working for many years voluntarily and professionally within both disability sport and education, this gave me an ideal opportunity to take part in a sailing activity where I could experience working aboard a sailing ship, while at the same time, helping people with disabilities achieve their own ambitions of going to sea. Both these remarkable ships sail out of the United Kingdom on voyages into the North Sea, the West European Basin, the Atlantic Ocean, the Caribbean and the Mediterranean Sea. Each ship's complement consists of a permanent crew of four deck officers, two engineers, a medical purser and cook and several volunteers acting as bosun's mates, watchleaders, doctor and assistant cook, with the remainder of the ship's company

The ship's bell. Launched in 2000, the Tenacious *was the second sailing vessel built by the Jubilee Sailing Trust. The first,* Lord Nelson, *sailed on its maiden voyage in 1986.*

comprising of forty crewmembers, half of whom have a sensory or a physical disability.

The chance to sail with the Jubilee Sailing Trust was too good an opportunity to miss, so I signed up for a voyage on the three masted barque *Tenacious*, launched in 2000 and the largest wooden tall ship to be built in Britain for over 100 hundred years. Measuring just over 213 feet long, including the bowsprit, the ship has a beam of thirty-four feet, a draft of fifteen feet and a mainmast measuring

123 feet high. With a displacement of 714 tonnes, the barque is comparable in size to a nineteenth-century square rigger. The *Tenacious* was designed by Tony Castro and built by professional shipwrights together with able-bodied and physically disabled volunteers at the Jubilee Yard at Merlin Quay in Southampton. Using the latest techniques of gluing and laminating the ship's timbers, sawn from Siberian Larch, this was the first time such a method had been used in the construction of a hull for a vessel of such size. The deckhouses were all built in wood and aluminium, with the masts built of steel and yards of aluminium. The ship's masts carried twenty-one sails, totalling over 13,000 square foot of canvas. The crew's accommodation is divided out much as it would have been on both naval and merchant vessel from the age

A view looking down from the yards of Tenacious, *some 65 feet above sea level and only halfway up the ship's foremast.*

of sail, with the captain's cabin located furthest aft of the ship's poop deck and the cabins of the permanent crew and the ship's officers, situated aft on the upper deck. The remainder of the crew were accommodated on the lower deck forward and port and starboard amidships. The crew's main mess was located aft of the crew accommodation, with the galley and watch crew's mess on the upper deck forward of the poop house. The ship was equipped

with two 400 BHP diesel engines, a requirement for all newly built sailing vessels and are used to manoeuvre the ship in and out of port and to assist when sailing in light winds. The engines were positioned amidships, taking up an area which would have been used for storage of supplies and cargo on an eighteenth-century and nineteenth-century square rig ship. A majority of the funding to build the *Tenacious* came through a National Lottery grant, with the costs of the voyages subsidised through the charity's own fundraising activities.

The port of departure for my venture under sail was Poole in Dorset, where I arrived on a bright and sunny August morning making my way along the High Street, kit bag over my shoulder, towards the quay. Walking through the Old Town and along the aptly named Thames Street, I rounded the corner onto the waterfront to find the impressive looking square rigger tied up alongside the quay, with tall masts stretching up towards the clear blue sky and sunlight reflecting off the bright white paintwork. The ship had attracted a large crowd of onlookers, who seemed somewhat astounded to find such a stunning sailing ship moored up at the quay, which made me feel privileged to be sailing as a member of the crew.

Climbing the gangplank, I was met by a member of the permanent crew who directed me to one of the ship's four watchleaders aboard, who allocated members of the crew, whether experienced or a novice, one of four watches, forward-port, forward-starboard, aft-port and aft-starboard; my watch being forward-starboard. Each watch duty lasted for around four hours in every twelve hour period, rotating over seven watches during the twenty-four hour day. Watch duties included steering the ship, taking bearings, keeping lookout, raising and lowering the sails and setting the yards as well as the inevitable galley duties, washing up, laying tables and peeling the veg!

Once directed to stow my kit in a cabin on the lower deck, eight of which were equipped to accommodate wheelchair users, I was introduced to my buddy who previously sailed with the Jubilee Sailing Trust on the *Lord Nelson*. The cabin, which we were to share, was located starboard amid-ships and comprised of a bunk bed and a small fitted cupboard – no hammocks.

Left: Crew's cabin on the Tenacious, *consisting of two bunks and a small fitted cupboard to store clothing. During heavy seas the bunks are rigged up with a lee cloth, which prevents you falling out when the ship rolls.*

Right: Manning the yards and making the sails ready before leaving port. Both topsails and course sails on the main and foremast needed volunteers to go aloft to furl or unfurl them.

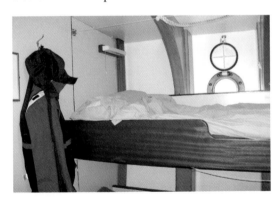

After all our paperwork had been checked, we were officially signed on as members of the crew, then allocated our wet weather gear, boots and safety harnesses, before taken to the mess for a full briefing prior to leaving port, which included safety precautions, man overboard procedures and sailing and seamanship duties. Throughout the voyage, when not on watch, all the crew would be required to help with deck duties, which included climbing up to the yards to furl and unfurl the sails on the main and forward masts. Everyone one was given the opportunity to climb up to the yards before departure if they felt up to it. The thought of climbing up into the rigging was quite daunting at first, however with safety harnesses on, I made it to the foretop, climbing aloft up the ratlines, wooden bars and ropes which make a ladder up to the yards, which was not as difficult as I first expected. However with the ship fairly motionless tied up along shore, climbing up to the yards under sail, especially if sailing in heavy weather, would be another matter.

Left: *Ship's mess, where the array of provisions provided were more plentiful and healthier than crews would have found aboard sailing vessels during the seventeenth and eighteenth centuries, there was no chance of contracting scurvy on the* Tenacious.

Right: *Taking a turn at the wheel. Each watch member spent part of the watch steering the ship, following course directions issued by the officer of the watch.*

Before leaving port I was given the duty of acting as one of the ship's linemen, which required remaining ashore with five other crew members to let go the ship's mooring lines, then once the vessel had made way, catching up with *Tenacious* in the ship's RIB, rigid inflatable boat, climbing aboard up a rope ladder with the ship well underway. The RIB was then hoisted aboard and stowed away amidships on top of the deckhousing.

By late afternoon, the ship had made its way out to sea, heading across the English Channel and south-west towards Cap De La Hague. Although my watch were not on duty until 8.00 p.m., all the crew were kept busy setting the sails after first briefed on rope handling, sailing terminology and the ship's sail plan. Dinner was then served at 6.00 p.m., where the rations on offer would have seemed like a banqueting feast for mariners sailing on the tall ships of the past. The *Tenacious* even had a small self service bar on the mess deck, opened during the early evening where the maritime tradition of taking a daily supply of alcoholic beverage was available if so desired, although several members of the crew declined this opportunity on the first day out at sea, suffering from the same condition as Lord

Forward starboard watch making ready the buntlines of the fore lower topsail. The array of lines laid out port, starboard, forward and aft of the ship controlled all the sails and held up the masts and yards. Confusing at first, by the end of the voyage the new crew members, myself included, all knew the difference between buntlines, sheets, furling lines and halyards.

Horatio Nelson himself while serving aboard ship, sea sickness.

During my first watch duty I had an opportunity to helm *Tenacious* under sail, which is basically steering the ship on a required course, indicated by a compass forward of the ship's wheel. Taking course directions from the officer on watch, one of the permanent crew, the wheel is turned to port or starboard, which changes the angle of the rudder, bringing the ship to bear on the required course heading, which needed a lot of concentration as it was easy to over or under steer this huge ship. Once on a steady course you then needed to ensure the ship did not drift off the required course due to any changes in the strength and direction of the wind and the currents. Every hour, a member of the watch made a record in the ship's log of the course steered, wind direction, ship's speed, distance travelled, sea conditions and air pressure. Throughout the four-hour watch each watch member on duty took a turn at the helm, while the remainder took bearings and kept lookout, scanning the sea and the horizon for any shipping or buoys coming into sight, which were reported to the watchleader or officer on the bridge. After your watch was through, you were then able to take some free time out, or take to your bunk for a period of sleep, which on the first night I found extremely difficult as the ship was pitching and rolling around as the wind picked up to force-seven during the early hours of the morning. At breakfast, served at 8.00 a.m., the bountiful servings of bacon, egg, sausages, beans and fried bread was well received by some of the new recruits, but turned down by others, preferring some toast and a strong cup of tea. For myself I was fortunate not to have suffered from serious bouts of sea sickness, a resilience I may have inherited through my ancestral seafairing roots or most likely through the times I used to go sea fishing out into the English Channel in some very heavy weather conditions. For one hour each day, usually in the morning, the crew of the ship were involved in what is commonly known aboard as

Happy hour aboard Tenacious, with brushes in hand members of the crew ready themselves to scrub the decks.

'Happy Hour', a terminology which does not accurately reflect the duties required, which is actually an hour spent cleaning the ship throughout, decks, cabins, brass and woodwork. Afterwards came 'Smoko', half an hour of leisure time where the crew were issued with as much tea, coffee and cake as you could consume.

After passing around Alderney, heading towards the Channel Islands, we encountered a small yacht sailing towards our position on a heading which would take the boat aft of our stern to port. As the yacht closed in we saw several dolphins dipping in and out of the water riding on the boats bow-wave as it passed us by. One of the permanent crew told that when the *Tenacious* was running along at a good speed, it was not unusual for dolphins and porpoises to ride the ship's own bow-wave when sailing out in the waters of the English Channel. Throughout the voyage everyone aboard was able to play an active part in sailing this magnificent tall ship, where each member of the crew was assigned duties which met each person's individual ability and strengths. A great camaraderie built up between the crew and we were all well supported by the permanent crew, most of whom were seafaring professionals earning their living working in the maritime industry. Our captain for the voyage had made the merchant navy her career and earned a masters certificate in 1999.

Sailing on southwards, the Channel Islands were sighted on the horizon and the ship made course for Jersey where we would spend the night in port. Shortly before our arrival, a few miles off shore, a local pilot came aboard to take the ship into St Helier and I was once again given the duty of acting as one of the linemen, going ashore in the RIB to await the ship's arrival. Once in the

Captain of Tenacious, *Barbara Campbell, on the ship's bridge with the St Helier pilot giving the helmsman instructions to take the ship safely through the harbour channel.*

Lineman duties, the RIB takes a member from each four watches ashore, with two of the permanent crew, to await the ship's arrival at the harbour of St Helier.

Sunset in the English Channel, the night before arriving at St Helier.

small harbour, the *Tenacious* was expertly manoeuvred alongside a jetty, where the crew aboard threw across the ship's forward, stern and spring lines, used to haul the heavy mooring ropes across to make the ship fast and secure. A majority of the crew took the opportunity to spend the evening on dry land for a meal and a few drinks, reminiscent of times gone by when the crews from sailing ships ventured ashore in distant and unfamiliar ports full of anticipation for how they may welcomed, with hospitality or hostility, although on this occasion the population of St Helier were more than friendly.

Once back out at sea, our duties aboard ship continued, raising sail, hauling rope, watch duty, happy hour, smoko, breakfast, lunch and dinner. During the evening we had some free time to have a drink of rum from the bar, while playing a game of 'Farkle', a dice game which, I was informed by my watchleader, originated in the Middle Ages and was apparently played on long voyages aboard sailing ships during the 1600s. After a couple more rounds, it would be off to your bunk for a well earned rest, unless you were on middle-watch. I found both the first-watch, 8.00 a.m. to midnight and the middle-watch, midnight to 4.00 a.m., two of the best watches to be on duty through, especially during the night with only the ship's navigation and deck safety lights illuminating the ship in a soft red, green and yellow glow. During my very first watch at night, there was a light breeze blowing, where the only sails set to catch the wind were the upper and lower topsails, the course sail on the foremast and the upper and lower topsail on the mainmast, which moved the ship smoothly and almost silently through open water. Looking up into the blackness above, where millions of pinpoints of bright light filled the night sky, it was not too difficult to let my imagination take me back to a time when ships were navigated by using the position of those same stars.

Author on the ship's bowsprit getting ready for first watch, 8.00 p.m. to midnight.

Forward starboard watch raising sail on the ship's foremast, carried out with almost expert precision, under guidance of the bosun's mate.

175

The captain of the *Tenacious* had so far not had an opportunity to give the order to raise all of the ship's square sails, however, during the following morning as soon as conditions were favourable, all hands were called up on deck to make ready for bracing the yards and setting the sails. With the crew taking up their four-watch positions forward and aft, all the ship's square sails on both the

Making ready to hoist a crew member up to the foretop, a platform on the foremast where wheelchair users could experience what it was like to go aloft.

Haul away; safely strapped into a special harness, the wheelchair user rises some 60 feet up above the deck.

fore and mainmast were set, along with the main topmast staysail, carried out with workmanlike precision by the crew. As the winds changed throughout the voyage, the ship's sails were raised and set to make best use of the weather conditions and during calm periods, crew members who were not on watch took the chance of climbing the ratlines on their own, up to the top of the fore or mainmast, to get a spectacular view from high above. Those aboard who were wheelchair users, or required assistance in climbing aloft, had an opportunity to try it for themselves during the voyage. A type of boson's chair was fitted to the wheelchair, which fully supported the users weight and then when strapped in by a safety harness, we all hauled on a line to lift them smoothly upwards to the fore top platform. One young wheelchair user was not too keen at first to try this out, however after watching another wheelchair user have a go and deciding he did not want miss out on this extraordinary opportunity, he was soon aloft taking photographs from the fore top platform.

Going aloft again myself, while the ship was now under sail, I could really appreciate the courage it took for those of my crewmates, who were apprehensive about going aloft, making it to the fore top platform with the assistance of ever helpful permanent crew. For many of those sailing aboard the *Tenacious* and the *Lord Nelson*, the voyages can be life-changing experiences, not only for those sailing who have sensory and physical disabilities, but also for

Looking aft from the end of the ship's bowsprit, standing on netting with nothing else but the sea below.

those who go along to act as buddies and volunteers, which is well described by Ian Shuttleworth, a Trustee and wheelchair user who wrote the JST brochure,

'The tall ships experience provides a wonderful, friendly and life enhancing opportunity for people of all physical abilities to work together on board our ships, gain self-confidence, push individual boundaries and be valued for what one can do, not what one can't.'

Ship's complement, the permanent crew, volunteer watch leaders and regular crew at St Helier August 2011.

Although there may be many other sailing organisations offering all types of experiences and adventures at sea, my own time aboard the *Tenacious* not only gave me an insight in what life is like working and living aboard a tall ship, it also offered me an opportunity to support others aboard who would not have been able to have a chance to participate in such a sailing adventure if it were not for the Jubilee Sailing Trust, the permanent crew of both ships and the volunteers who sail with these fantastic vessels. For myself I felt

Above: *Crewmembers' logbook with the Jubilee Sailing Trust official stamp for completing a voyage.*

Above left: *Forward starboard watch left to right, Daniel Goodman, Joseph Goodman, watchleader Jenny Wedick, Helen Atkins, David Ramzan, Elizabeth Hedges and Stephen Kitson.*

Left: *The ship's muster list for voyage 320, with the crew totalling forty-one. On longer voyages the* Tenacious *can accommodate fifty-two crew members.*

Total on Board	41

MUSTER LIST   VOYAGE 320
Tenacious
VOYAGE CREW

FWD PORT

28	Stuart Sheldon
10	Joanna Mercer
43	Janet Cox
45	Sheonagh Ravensdale
6	Patricia Thompson
14	Rebecca O'neil
17	Courtney Buchanan
19	Conner O'donavon

FWD STARBOARD

36	Jenny Wedick
33	David Ramzan
31	Stephen Kitson
	Helen Allkins
38	Elizabeth Hedges
3	Daniel Goodman
1	Joseph Goodman

AFT PORT

13	Mike Bartlett
11	Michael Hilton
9	Alex Farrow
35	Jonathan Morley
21	Greg Jones
22	Debbie Tottingham
37	Clive Morley
5	Kevin Bennet

AFT STARBOARD

2	Denise Speirs
42	Susan Williams
40	Bridget Le Huray
39	Hannah Rose
41	Pauline Curling
44	Leslie Ball
46	Claudia Mansey

PERMANENT CREW

CAPTAIN	Barbara Campbell		MED. PURSER	Ronan Ging
MATE	John Hissey		COOK	Elizabeth Tappenden
2nd MATE	Alex Fogarty	27	Cook's Assistan	Sharon Haigh
BOSUN	Matt Smith		Supernum. MP	Helen Allkins
C. ENGINEER	Pete Stonehouse	32	BOSUN'S MATE	Samantha Kendall
2nd ENGINEER	Tony Heard	30	BOSUN'S MATE	Laurie O'Calaghan

179

extremely fortunate to have sailed as part of the crew on Britain's largest timber-built sailing ship the *Tenacious*.

Although none of the wooden ships built in Britain during the age of sail – East Indiamen, warship and clipper – are no longer raising sail on the open sea, both the *Victory* and *Cutty Sark*, the two most famous survivors from these historic nautical times, are now land-locked and enclosed in dry docks. The remains of ships lost at sea, such as the wreck of the *Mary Rose*, have been raised from where they sank and after a preservation process, have been exhibited in museums. All of the ships built in the Royal Dockyards at Deptford and Woolwich and at the iron shipyard on Greenwich Marsh, were either shipwrecked or sunk during service, or broken up once their useful sailing days were over.

The remains of the East Indiaman *Princess Louisa*, which lay on the sea bed of Galleons Reef for over 250 years, were discovered by a team of Portuguese aqua-nautical archaeological divers in 1998, where the wreck was plotted at 15°17,7 latitude, 23°04,7 longitude. The finds included ivory tusks, guns, anchors, pewter plates, cutlery, glass bottles – some full – and the most precious cargo of all; the hoard of Spanish silver reales from the Company's thirty chests of treasure. Many of the silver reales contained within the chests were by then in poor condition, contaminated from the copper content in the silver, with hundreds of coins fused together in large rock-hard clumps of sediment. The silver reales which were salvageable and

HMS Victory at Portsmouth. The great oak-built man-of-war became a sail training ship during the early 1900s before installed in dry dock as a permanent maritime museum in 1922.

are now extremely valuable, have been restored and can now be purchased individually or mounted into presentation cases which all come with letters of authenticity. Although the actual remains of the East Indiaman have now long gone, you can still own a piece of treasure from the *Princess Louisa*.

There is nothing left to be found of the Royal Naval ship *Dolphin*, which circumnavigated the globe on two occasions and fought against the enemies of Britain across all the oceans of the

Spanish Silver Reales were used to pay for goods and employees of the East India Company. Thousands of coins were found on the seabed where the Princess Louisa was wrecked upon the reef, which can now be purchased as souvenirs.

world. Perhaps somewhere along the Southbank of the Thames the remnants of the frigate's timbers may have been used in the construction of riverside buildings, docks or wharfs, even in the manufacture of furniture, as was the custom when ships' lives were over and the vessels were broken up. Perhaps one day the timbers of the *Dolphin* may be discovered during excavations taking place along the Thames riverside, such as the remains found during an archaeological dig at Bellamy Wharf, Rotherhithe, in 1995, where ships' timbers, believed to have come from the *Royal Oak* and *Loyal London*, had been used in the building of the dock.

As for the iron clipper ship *Hallowe'en*, wrecked at Sewer Mill Cove, all that remains of the last British-built tea clipper are a few of the ship's iron ribs and plates protruding out from the sands off-shore, which can often be seen when the tide is at its lowest. One of the clipper's brass port-lights was salvaged and has now been put on display at Salcombe

Maritime and Local History Museum in Devon, the only surviving remnant from a sailing ship built in the yards on Greenwich Marsh.

Even though the Greenwich shipbuilding industry finally came to a close at the beginning of the twentieth century, almost a hundred years on, one of the most famous tall ships of all time was undergoing a complete re-build in a dry dock at the town's centre; the last surviving authentic square rigged tea clipper, the *Cutty Sark*. While undergoing

Commemorative coins and stamps from islands in the Pacific, dedicated to the Dolphin's *circumnavigations around the world.*

multi-million pound renovations, this historic Greenwich tourist attraction, placed in a dry dock and opened to the public during the 1950s, caught fire in May 2007 and was severely damaged throughout. The cause of the fire was attributed to an industrial vacuum cleaner left connected to the mains, which then overheated and caught light during the night. Whilst a majority of the ship's decking and internal fittings had been removed for storage at Chatham Historic Dockyard, along with the ship's masts, yards and rigging, the inferno destroyed a majority of the ship's remaining timbers and seriously damaged the iron-work which made up the clipper's frame. The amount of work which needed to be carried out on the vessel was comparable to building the ship from new. On completion of the renovations and re-build, the *Cutty Sark* is sailing once more, although not on the ocean, but upon a sea of glass. The clipper has been suspended above the bottom of the dry dock with a canopy of glass acting as the water-line, giving an impression that the ship is afloat. Tourists are

Sewer Mill Cove, with the Ham Stone towards the left and the rising rocks of the cliffs to the right. In between lays the remains of the clipper Hallowe'en.

LIST OF SERVICES RENDERED BY THE

HOPE COVE LIFEBOAT

OF THE

ROYAL NATIONAL LIFEBOAT INSTITUTION

The 'ALEXANDRA' LIFEBOAT

1887	Jan. 18th	Ship "HALLOWEEN" of London	19
1896	Dec. 1st	Steamer "BLESK" of Odessa	43
1899	Oct. 26	Trawler "ALPHA" of Brixham Stood By VESSEL
1904	May 27	S.S. LADY HUDSON KINAHAN of Dublin
1907	Mar. 18th	S.S. JEBBA of London Stood By VESSEL
1911	Mar. 23	S.S. CARDIUM of London RENDERED ASSISTANCE
1912	Mar. 25th	Schooner "SIDNEY SMITH" of Portmadoc	2
1914	Feb. 28th	S.S. JANE ROWE of Goole Stood by VESSEL
	Mar. 1st	S.S. JANE ROWE of Goole Stood by VESSEL
1926	Feb. 15th	S.S. LIBERTA of Genoa. Stood by

Memorial plaque on display at the Hope & Anchor public house, Hope Cove, recording the list of rescues made by the lifeboat Alexandria, *between 1887 and 1926, with the* Hallowe'en *being the first.*

183

Above: *The hull of the rebuilt clipper*
Cutty Sark *takes shape, with the
superstructure of the glass canopy
above the visitor centre under
construction during 2011.*

Right: *Figure head of the* Cutty Sark
*'Nannie' back in place awaiting the for
the clipper's completion.*

able to walk under the glass, under the hull of the very last sailing
ship to be built (or re-built) at Greenwich, once the centre of
British shipbuilding. Previous to the Millennium celebrations in
Greenwich, which took place at the beginning of the year 2000,
the whole area along the length of the River Thames from the Pool
of London to the Isle of Dogs, the docklands, Greenwich Marsh
and beyond, had begun to fall under the developer's hammer,
where vast areas of historical industrial landscape were flattened,

Above: *The clipper in all its glory, opened to the public in April 2012.*

Left: *Bow of the clipper below the waterline where the entire ship's hull, sheathed in copper, is now protected from the elements under a vast glass canopy.*

The Pool of London and Tower Bridge with Butlers Wharf to the left, which once contained the largest tea warehouses in the world.

replaced by offices, apartments, modern industrial estates, hotels, restaurants, shopping centres and leisure facilities. A few listed buildings and original warehouses along the river and in the docklands were retained, transformed into retail, living, or work places. People who are now moving into the area are unlikely to know of London's shipping and shipbuilding heritage.

Oliver's Wharf, Wapping, on the north bank of the Thames. Built in 1869 the warehouse stored shipments of tea.

Top: *The remains of one of the Woolwich Royal Dockyard slips, nestling in between two residential apartment blocks.*

Below: *The area once occupied by the Deptford shipbuilding yards, under complete regeneration.*

On the site of the Royal Dockyards at Deptford, now known as Convoys Wharf, there are controversial plans underway to turn the 40 acre area into a vast new development to include residential, commercial, retail and leisure facilities. The developers, in consultation with archaeologists and the local council, propose to retain some of the few existing features of the site. However, this will amount to not much more than some dockyard foundation works, filled in slipways and basins, the existing Victorian Olympic Slip Shed, water frontage and a twentieth-century built jetty. The proposed commercial area may include facilities for light-industrial usage, where one project could bring shipbuilding back to Deptford once more. A group of enthusiasts are proposing to build a replica of the Restoration warship *Lenox* in the dockyard, which at the present has no working links to its shipbuilding past, where this ship was originally built and launched in 1678.

Launch of Lenox *at Deptford on 12 April 1678 attended by King Charles and Louise De Keroualle, Duchess of Portsmouth and their son Charles Lenox after whom the ship was named.*

On Greenwich Marsh, which continues to undergo a process of regeneration and change, there is nothing to record the ship and boatbuilding industry which thrived on the Marsh for more than 200 years. Perhaps in time this will change and the ships which were built at the Royal Dockyards and on Greenwich Marsh will also receive the recognition they deserve for the parts each played in British maritime history.

Bay Wharf, site of the Maudslay shipbuilding yards at an area of Greenwich Marsh awaiting development. There have been plans to relocate a Greenwich boat yard from its current site west along the river to Bay Wharf, which may revive the area's boat and ship building heritage.

Acknowledgements

Many of the images produced in this publication have come from my own collection, which I have compiled over many years, from photographs I have taken and illustrations I have created. I should also like to acknowledge all those individuals and organisations who have contributed images and historical information included within this publication. If for any reason I have not accredited use of images and information to persons or organisations as necessary, or failed to trace any copyright holders, then I should like to apologise for any oversight and for any inadvertent omissions to the list below.

Alison Crowther, Cutty Sark Trust. British Library. Caird Library & National Maritime Museum at Greenwich. Captain Cook Museum at Whitby. Crimosteve. David Foker. Richard Endsor & Julian Kingston - Build the Lenox. Devon Record Office. Dover Publications, Inc. Greenwich Heritage Centre. Greenwich Industrial Society. Hartlepool's Maritime Experience. Jenny Wedick. Jubilee Sailing Trust. Kingsbridge Cooksworthy Museum. Museum of London. Museum of London Dockyards. National Archives. Port of London Authority. RNLI at Salcombe. Royal Naval Museum at Portsmouth. Royal Observatory at Greenwich. Salcombe Maritime & Local History Museum. Tallshipstock.com. University of Houston Libraries. Families of Austin, Peachey, Ramzan and Robinson.

For all those salty seadogs who would like to find out more about sailing under canvas, or building a full-size wooden warship, I can recommend you contact the Jubilee Sailing Trust and Build the Lenox, two worthy organisations keeping seafaring history and heritage alive.

www.jst.org.uk
www.buildthelenox.org